Time Bomb
in the Middle East
Countdown to Armageddon

Time Bomb in the Middle East
Countdown to Armageddon

by
Dr. Lester Sumrall

Harrison House
Tulsa, Oklahoma

Unless otherwise indicated, all Scripture quotations are taken from the *King James Version* of the Bible.

Time Bomb in the Middle East —
Countdown to Armageddon
ISBN 0-89274-875-3
(Former Library of Congress Catalog
Card Number: 80-52479)
Copyright © 1991 by Lester Sumrall
   Evangelistic Association
P. O. Box 12
South Bend, Indiana

Published by Harrison House, Inc.
P. O. Box 35035
Tulsa, Oklahoma 74153

Contents

Foreword

The evidence is overwhelming!

Jesus is coming again!

The Middle East Crisis is one more powerful sign pointing the way.

The Russian Bear and its rebellious republics (many of which are Islamic) sit poised like a black widow spider — ready to pounce on its unsuspecting prey. The prize — the nation of Israel. Three million plus Jews are surrounded by more than 100 million hostile Arabs, most of them supported with Russian fire power. God's hook is set in the Russian jaw — she is being irresistibly drawn to that inevitable rendezvous where she shall be judged and most of her military power annihalated.

Dr. Sumrall has documented from the prophetic Word of God Iraq's and Iran's unique role in God's plan of the ages and the final drama of the Dispensation.

Now is the time for the Body of Christ to arise and reap the final harvest of immortal souls.

Now is the time to win our lost loved ones and neighbors. It will never be easier — God's Holy Spirit is active and moving in the world! Joel's prophecy is being fulfilled. The Spirit is falling in conviction upon all flesh. Body of Christ, let's get the job done now so that Jesus can return! Jesus said:

> **And when these things begin to come to pass, then look up, and lift your heads, for your redemption draweth nigh.**
>
> **Luke 21:28**

I commend this exciting book and Dr. Sumrall to you, knowing that you will be blessed and inspired to do your part in bringing back the King!

Paul F. Crouch
Trinity Broadcasting Network
Los Angeles, California

Preface

The world's attention was turned to the Middle East when Saddam Hussein ruthlessly occupied and terrorized his neighbor, the tiny emirate of Kuwait. This ancient region is a time bomb ready to explode. The circumstances leading to the future battle of Armageddon have been building for thousands of years — since the days of Abram and Lot. The modern-day conflict was begun by a religious Moslem dictator, Ayatolla Ruhollah Khomeini, the religious and political revolutionary for the Moslem world. He fully supported Yasar Arafat, the leader of the P.L.O. (Palestine Liberation Organization), and other Moslem hate group terrorists worldwide, their goal being the destruction of the State of Israel.

Khomeini, as an Imam, a Moslem Shiite leader, possessed tremendous wealth in land and gold. Saddam Hussein, meanwhile, was acquiring large oil revenues and Western and Soviet military might.

More importantly, the millions of dollars given to support Arafat by both of these men reveal that the holding of American hostages in Iran and Iraq was Jihad, the ancient Islamic declaration of Holy War. From reading Isaiah Chapter 10 in the Bible, we know that the Assyrian will have power.

Iraq and Iran are modern geographic locations. Much of Iran was formerly described as Persia, Media, and Elam. Iraq in antiquity was called Babylon, Assyria, Mesopotamia, Shinar, and Arabia. Keep in mind that these names all refer to geographic locations and not particularly to races of mankind that lived there. The Assyrians, Medes, Chaldeans, Elamites, Persians, Babylonians, Jews, Armenians, Kurds, and many other races were always living in these two regions and helped form the Babylonian and Persian Empires mentioned in history.

Iraq and Iran, with 4,000 years of recorded history, give us the best vantage point to observe the ultimate destiny of the peoples of the region as revealed in the world's most reliable textbook — the Bible. We must learn from history — the history revealed in the Bible.

To be ignorant of the religious convictions of Yasar Arafat, the Ayatollah Khomeini, and Saddam Hussein is dangerous, religiously, economically, and politically.

Jerusalem is the center and heartbeat of the Middle East crisis. The Jihad hopes to draw the whole world into this bloody vortex of prophetical warfare.

We will see in this book that we are now in the final countdown of the Almighty God to the Battle of Armageddon. What will people do about God's final countdown? Will they turn to Him? Enoch did, and God translated him to Heaven. Noah did, and God preserved him in the great ark.

The best way people can prepare for the countdown is to give their heart to the Lord Jesus Christ. He will lead them to a place of salvation; He will lead them to a place of safety; He will lead them to a place of security: and that can be only in the Almighty God when someone confesses Jesus as their Lord and Savior.

Follow this lesson closely, and be on the side of Jesus in these strategic moments of the final countdown to Armageddon.

Time Bomb
in the Middle East
Countdown to Armageddon

1
Ancient Babylon
Rises Again

On January 15, 1991, under the operational name of "Desert Storm," and in response to Iraq's invasion of Kuwait five months before, United States and Coalition planes began their assault on Baghdad. As war began in the Middle East, the attention of the world was turned to the conflict in the Persian Gulf. From the Western perspective, it was a war opposing aggression and a war for control of the world's oil reserves. From the perspective of Islamic Arabs, it was Jihad, the Holy War.

Battle lines have been drawn between Saddam Hussein and Coalition forces. But it is not just Iraq who is drawing battle lines. Several Moslem nations are rising up in public protest against the presence of Western military forces, especially American, in the Gulf nations. The cry is being heard throughout the world: "Jihad, Jihad, the Holy War! Death to all infidels! Death to all Israel! Death to all Jews! Death to America, the Great Satan!"

Even though the United States government views the Arab-Israeli conflict as a separate issue, the truth of the matter is that the war in the Middle East and the Arab-Israeli conflict are one and the same. The invasion of Kuwait was just a means to an end. It was part of Saddam Hussein's strategy to draw all Arab nations into a Jihad against Israel and her allies.

Preachers fill their pulpits, proclaiming that the end of this age is upon us according to Biblical prophecy. Evangelists and ministers are on the news and talk shows speaking of imminent destruction. Church attendance is at an all time high, as people turn to their church leaders for answers.

With anticipation of even greater disaster on the horizon, some ask:

"Is this Armageddon?"

"Is this the beginning of the end?"

"Are Saddam Hussein and the Iraqi war predicted in the Bible?"

"Why is there hatred toward the United States?"

"Why is the United States viewed as 'The Great Satan'?"

"What is the future of Israel, Iraq and the Moslem world?"

These are questions in the minds of Christians everywhere as the world is torn by war and the end seems nearer than ever before. I will address these questions and others as we look at the current situation in the Persian Gulf from a Biblical and historical perspective.

The Beginnings of the Conflict

The conflict with Iraq did not start in August 1990 with the invasion of Kuwait. Nor did it start with Israelis occupying Palestinian territory. Rather, the conflict began centuries ago. What we are viewing on our television screens every night in our living rooms in the fulfillment of Biblical prophecies made centuries ago.

Iraq is located geographically on the ruins of ancient Babylon, the first world empire. The greed and lust for power that was manifested in Nebuchadnezzar when he ruled ancient Babylon is seen again in Saddam Hussein. He can personally murder his own friends, burn his own citizens with chemicals and poison gas and rain missles on innocent civilians in Israel and Saudi Arabia. Death and murder control him.

The Western mind of England and America find Saddam Hussein a mystery. Is he just another tyrant like Hitler, bent on building a personal empire, or is his life part of a larger picture found in prophecy? For sure, the United Nations knew that a madman from ancient Babylon must not control sixty-five percent of the world's oil reserves.

But greed and lust for power have always been with us. The question in the minds of many is, how is this conflict different from others of history, and how does it fit in with the plan of God for the end of this age?

In this book I take you on a historical journey, showing from Scripture the roots of the people of the Middle East and why they are so intent on preserving and expanding their influence and rule, even when thousands of lives may be sacrificed in the process.

2

America, the Great Satan?

In some parts of the world, America is referred to as "The Great Satan" and seen as an evil force in the earth. The Ayatollah Khomeni often referred to the U.S. as "The Great Satan." Now Saddam Hussein and some Moslem clerics throughout the Middle East are echoing that cry again. Why is this so? What sparked the outrage in much of the world against America and the Western nations?

Recently one of our staff personnel was ministering in the Moslem nation of Turkey. He lived among the Turks and had many opportunities to talk with Moslem holy men. When he asked them why there is such widespread hatred for America and a belief that it is satanic in nature, they told him it is because America is viewed as deceitful and hyprocritical. One Moslem cleric stated that on the one hand Americans carry the gospel of love and truth, and preach eternal life, but very often on the other hand bring immorality, corruption and sin.

To Moslems, the church and state are inseparable, because the state passes laws that affect public morals. According to Moslem doctrine, to say that there is a separation between church and state is merely hypothetical and can never operate in fact.

To Moslem thinking, the church and state are incapable of being separated, and religion and government must be tied together as one. Because of this reasoning, they view America as a Christian nation, whether or not individuals within America believe that of America.

Since America is viewed as a Christian nation, Moslems assume that the actions of America, its government and citizens should reflect Christian ideals and principles. Yet they see America as the number one promoter of immorality and perversion around the world.

As an example, many Moslem nations feel their society has been invaded with pornographic magazines, immoral movies and rock music, all of which they see as promoting sin and destruction. They are concerned with the drug culture and crime problems they see in America and believe those problems are being exported into their countries.

Because America is both good and evil, in their opinion we must be a devil and terribly deceived. Because of this deception, Americans and most other westerners are considered "infidels" or "servants of the devil." Because America is hyprocritical and cannot control its lusts, greed and evil ways, many Moslems believe it should be destroyed.

It is interesting to note in light of the above what the prophet Isaiah said centuries ago about the people that make up modern-day Iraq and Iran:

> **Oh Assyrian, the rod of mine anger, and the staff in their hand is mine indignation. I will send him against an hypocritical nation, and against the people of my wrath will I give him a charge, to take the spoil,**

and to take the prey, (Kuwait) and to tread them down like the mire of the streets.

Isaiah 10:5,6

The religion of the present-day Assyrians is Islam, and this passage could help explain why Moslems are so intent on the destruction of America and the West.

Another example the Moslem holy men gave to our staff member to explain their feelings toward America is the Moslem view of eschatology, or the study of end-time prophecies. The Moslems believe in a coming world dictator similiar to the "Antichrist" talked about in the New Testament. In the Moslem view, this evil dictator will be a "one-eyed beast" who will dominate the world in economics, religion and military might. The one power today that Moslems believe is dominating the world in these areas is the United States; therefore, they equate America with the "one-eyed beast."

Adding to this aggravation, one Islamic holy man pointed out that on the back of a U.S. dollar bill is the pyramid/cabalist symbol used by Zionism and various cults. Atop that symbol is the all-seeing eye or one-eyed beast that Moslems believe will control the world with evil. The religious leader said that Moslems believe this symbol on the American dollar bill represents or is indicitive of this beastly system and that Allah, their god, wants it destroyed from the face of the earth. The Latin words under this pyramid symbol translates into "A New World Order." So when President Bush starts talking about a new world order following the Gulf War, many Moslems respond with a fever pitch of militant anger.

15

We can see from these two examples why many Moslems view the United States as "The Great Satan," particularly when they can see the American dollar being spent everywhere in the world. To a dedicated Moslem, that is a sure sign that the American dollar is representative of the beastly system of evil that God wants to destroy.

Understanding the way Moslems think toward America shows again how the devil can use religious systems to manipulate and control their followers into hatred, anger, terrorism, murder and all out war in the name of a holy and righteous cause. The concept of one world religion established by military conquest is drilled into the heads of many Moslems from infancy. They are taught to believe that the best way to die is in defending their faith, which will transport them immediately to heaven. Such fanatical zeal is largely unknown to the western mind. It often results in throwing out all the established rules of diplomacy and warfare, leaving only a barbarous fight to the finish, with the winner taking all.

Islamic View of Jesus

The concept of Jesus Christ as the liberator of men's souls is not understood in Islam. Moslems believe that Jesus was merely a prophet, one of six major prophets in the history of the world, of which Elijah Mohammed was the last and final authority.

The Koran, Islam's holy book, states, "God forbid that God should have a son." The Moslem believes that Jesus was a great prophet of the past and that He will return to rule the earth for a thousand years as God's servant and prophet, but not as His son. The

Arabic word "rueb," or "spirit," is used to describe a spirit of God living in Jesus Christ, but to them, Jesus is not the Son of God. He was only a great prophet possessed by the Spirit of God.

Moslems teach that Jesus existed in the past and will exist in the future, but He does not exist now. We as Christians know that Jesus Christ is God in the flesh, that He existed before all time and exists now as the bodily representation of the Godhead.(John 1:1.)

Just as He told Moses at the burning bush to tell the people "I AM" has sent you (Ex. 3:14), so our relationship with Christ now is a living experience with a real person existing in our spirits.

By saying that Jesus lived in the past and will come in the future denies the reality of Jesus in the present. A relationship with Jesus would not be possible if He did not live in the present. It is in the present that people need to live and have the power to overcome. For these reasons we can see that Islam is a spirit of antichrist in doctrine. Thus Islam has a form of godliness and righteousness, acknowledging much Biblical law and principle, but denies the transforming power of the risen Jesus Christ Who changes the heart of man from within. (2 Tim. 3:5.)

Because of this great deception of Satan, Christians should be expending a much greater effort to reach the Moslem world and bring the reality and power of Jesus Christ to this major portion of the world's population. Only then will this ancient rivalry between Isaac, the forefather of the Israelis, and Ishmael, the forefather of the Arabs, be resolved.

3
A Foundation
for War

The modern world was shocked when television, newspapers, and radio broadcast bulletins of the captured Embassy of the United States of America on November 4, 1979, and took hostage 63 citzens of one of the earth's greatest nations. It was Jihad.

Knowledgeable students of Bible prophecy were the least surprised at that terrible intrusion. They had been watching for a move from these ancient lands, for neither Iran, Iraq, nor the Islamic world, can escape their past history or future destiny.

You're not a student of Bible prophecy, you say? How can you know what to expect from Iran and the Moslem world?

My purpose in writing this book is to help you to know. Trace with me the history of Iran through the pages of the Bible. It isn't difficult to do. It isn't hidden. It isn't beyond your grasp. In fact, you will be fascinated at how your understanding of current world events widens in the light of God's Holy Word.

Iraq/Iran: Ancient Lands
Iran — called Persia until 1935 when it was renamed by its then Shah — has nearly 4,000 years of recorded and known history.

Iraq — the story begins with Noah's grandson, Elam.

But let's go back to the beginning — the beginning of man.

Adam, the first human, knew God on a very personal, one-to-one basis. Adam walked and talked with God. Adam knew how to worship the "Elohim" God in an acceptable manner. But Adam fell and mankind with him. This was approximately 6,000 years ago.

Some 2,000 years after the Eden catastrophe, only Noah knew God on a one-to-one basis. He preached and prepared for the deluge God told him would cover the earth. No one, outside his family, believed.

What a treasure was carried in the Ark that saved them! It was mankind's knowledge of God.

At this point in time, Noah and his family were the only Homo sapiens on the planet earth. They knew the true God and worshipped Him.

Noah's sons — Shem, Ham, and Japeth — left the Ark with a tremendous respect for the living God and divine order. They heard the voice of God and witnessed the birth of the rainbow — God's promise not to destroy the earth again with water. They stood at Noah's altar with heads bowed as the God of the universe promised there would never be another worldwide flood. They heard God's promise of perpetual seedtime and harvest.

Shem, Ham, and Japeth also remembered how wickedly the people lived who were destroyed by the flood.

What a tremendous memory bank! What knowledge to pass on from these three fathers to their offspring — the entire world's population!

Iraq/Iran and Early Bible History

Bible genealogy after the flood is found in Genesis chapters 10 and 11.

To Shem — Noah's son — Elam, Asshur, Arphaxad, Lud, and Aram were born. (Gen. 10:22.)

Elam became a tribe, built cities, ultimately vanquished Babylon, and became the Persian empire. Iran's and Iraq's histories are traceable through Elam.

Elam was at least one year older than his brother, Arphaxad. It is in Arphaxad's line that we find Abraham only ten generations from Noah's flood.

1. **Shem.**   **Noah begat three sons, Shem, Ham, and Japeth** (Gen. 6:10).

2. **Arphaxad.** **Shem was an hundred years old, and begat Arphaxad two years after the flood** (Gen. 11:10).

3. **Salah.**   **And Arphaxad lived five and thirty years, and begat Salah** (v. 12).

4. **Eber.**   **And Salah lived thirty years, and begat Eber** (v. 14).

5. **Peleg.**   **And Eber lived four and thirty years, and begat Peleg** (v. 16).

6. **Reu.**   **And Peleg lived thirty years, and begat Reu** (v. 18).

7. **Serug.**   **And Reu lived two and thirty years, and begat Serug** (v. 20).

8. Nahor.   **And Serug lived thirty years, and begat Nahor** (v. 22).

9. Terah.   **And Nahor lived nine and twenty years, and begat Terah** (v. 24).

10. Abram (Abraham). **And Terah lived seventy years, and begat Abram, Nahor, and Haran** (v. 26).

During these ten generations, many left the truths of God and began to serve idols.

These relatively few years witnessed the Tower of Babel and the dispersion of the nations by language. (Gen. 11:3-9.) In order for God to preserve the promised Seed of the woman and fulfill His prophecy given at the Garden of Eden (Gen. 3:15), He had to separate men — evil from good. God did this by confusion of language at Babel.

These years also witnessed, in the days of Peleg, the division of the earth from one land mass into continents and islands. (Gen. 10:25.) God again separated the good, God-fearing people from the rest of mankind. This was His means of bringing the world a Savior, Jesus Christ.

Less than 400 years after the flood, God spoke to Abram on a one-to-one basis and told him to leave Ur of the Chaldees — the area where the Assyrian, Babylonian, and Persian empires would later spring up.

It was Elamite raids that destroyed Ur about 1950 B.C.

4

The War Between
Israel and Iraq/Iran

It was Jehovah God who spoke to Abraham and caused him to leave Ur of the Chaldees, a place where many worshiped idols and demon spirits — the general area which would become Elam, Iraq, Persia and Iran.

The story of the flood had now passed through ten generations.

Now don't look at the Bible with vast distances. I hold in my experience knowledge of five generations. I remember my grandfather well; I know my grandchildren well. Some people remember great grandparents and live to know great grandchildren.

In only ten generations after Noah, in order to separate evil from good, God demanded Abraham to depart from Ur of the Chaldees.

Jehovah's divine guidance led him north to Haran across the desert into Canaan which was to become his homeland and the "Promised Land" to him and his seed after him.

In the land of Canaan Abraham continued to serve the true God of Noah and Adam.

He had amazing increase in his possessions.

> **Abram was very rich in cattle, in silver, and in gold.**
>
> **Genesis 13:2**

And so was his nephew, Lot, whom he had brought along with him.

> And Lot also, which went with Abram, had flocks, and herds, and tents. And the land was not able to bear them, that they might dwell together; for their substance was great, so that they could not dwell together.
>
> Genesis 13:5,6

The two could no longer live within the same grazing space for their cattle. They had to separate. But the land was great before them. Abraham gave Lot his choice saying,

> If thou wilt take the left hand, then I will go to the right; or if thou depart to the right hand, then I will go to the left.
>
> Verse 9

Lot chose the well-watered plain of Jordan. Journeying eastward he pitched his tent toward the city of Sodom where there was exceeding sin. Eventually, he moved into that wicked city and became an official in the city gate of Sodom.

Several years after Lot left Abraham, Sodom was besieged and captured by the kings of the Fertile Crescent.

> It came to pass in the days of Amraphel king of Shinar, Arioch king of Ellasar, Chedorlaomer king of Elam, and Tidal king of nations; that these made war with Bera king of Sodom, and with Birsha king of Gomorrah, Shinab king of Admah, and Shemeber king of Zeboiim, and the king of Bela, which is Zoar. All these were joined together in the vale of Siddim, which is the salt sea.
>
> Genesis 14:1-3

In this first recorded war in the Bible, we note Chedorlaomer, king of Elam. He was the leader of a coalition of kings from the same area Abraham had departed at God's command.

For twelve years the five principal cities in the Jordan plain, including Sodom and Gomorrah, had been made to serve Chedorlaomer and pay him tribute.

In the thirteenth year, the cities of the plain rebelled.

In the fourteenth year, the confederacy of kings headed up by the king of Elam came to put down the insurrection.

They smote Sodom and Gomorrah and took all their goods, their victuals, and many of their people as hostages. (Iran has been taking hostages for a long time.) Among their captives was Abraham's nephew, Lot.

Word of the capture reached Abraham. Someone who escaped the battle came with the news to Mamre where Abraham dwelled.

Abraham took three hundred and eighteen servants of his own house, armed them, and pursued the invading kings from Hebron in the south, through the hills of Judea, across Megiddo, up through the hills of Galilee, to Dan where he overtook them. A long pursuit!

Abraham divided his band and attacked by night. Then he chased the kings to Hobnah, north of Damascus, where he completely destroyed them.

He destroyed the powers of Persia in one night!

Genesis 14:17 tells how the king of Sodom came out to meet Abraham **after his return from the slaughter of Chedorlaomer and of the kings that were with him.**

Abraham brought Sodom's riches back to them and gave his nephew, Lot, his life.

Within a few years' time, Abraham had to fight the people of Elam where he had come from as a young man. God gave him power over the kings from his homeland. This is witnessed by Melchizedek's blessing when he met Abraham upon his return from the victory.

> **And Melchizedek king of Salem brought forth bread and wine; and he was the priest of the most high God. And he blessed him, and said, Blessed be Abram of the most high God, possessor of heaven and earth: And blessed by the most high God, which hath delivered thine enemies into thy hand. And he gave them tithes of all.**
>
> **Genesis 14:18-20**

The first step into Biblical history for Iran was when it faced the man of God, Abraham, and its king, Chedolaomer, was destroyed.

5

History Told
Before It Happened

Permit me to grasp your spirit so that we can walk together in the prophetical truth which will bring you an understanding of the times. For it is only through the Bible that anyone can understand them.

More than twenty-five hundred years ago, God spoke to a man named Daniel in visions and dreams and showed him empires unborn. History verifies the fact that this man prophesied the rise and fall of empires. Today you can see the blueprint of the future through this man of God named Daniel.

Daniel, a young prince of Judah, was carried off into captivity with other children of Israel by Nebuchadnezzar king of Babylon. There he was chosen, with other outstanding young captives, to be trained in the king's college for three years.

Daniel purposed in his heart to obey the living God. He would not defile himself with the king's meat or wine. Three fellow captives joined him.

God gave them favor and elevated them to high positions in the empire.

As for these four children, God gave them knowledge and skill in all learning and wisdom: and Daniel had understanding in visions and dreams. Now at the end of the days that the king had said he

27

should bring them in, then the prince of the eunuchs
brought them in before Nebuchadnezzar. And the
king communed with them; and among them all was
found none like Daniel, Hananiah, Mishael, and
Azariah; therefore stood they before the king. And
in all matters of wisdom and understanding, that the
king inquired of them, he found them ten times better
than all the magicians and astrologers that were in all
his realm.

Daniel 1:17-20

First Prophetic Picture
of Iraq/Iran: Silver

Daniel, through supernatural power, saw the
entire scope of world empires — but only those empires
prophetically involved with Christ — in three
revelations.

The first revelation initially came as a dream to the
worldly king, Nebuchadnezzar (Dan. 2:1-18).

The dream and its interpretation were revealed
unto Daniel in a night vision (Dan. 2:19).

Daniel said, in the presence of the king,

There is a God in heaven that revealeth secrets,
and maketh known to the king Nebuchadnezzar what
shall be in the latter days.

Daniel 2:28

Most believers know that we are in "the latter
days."

First Daniel told the king the dream.

Thou, O king, sawest, and behold a great image.
This great image, whose brightness was excellent,
stood before thee; and the form thereof was terrible.

This image's head was of fine gold, his breast and
his arms of silver, his belly and his thighs of brass,
his legs of iron, his feet part of iron and part of clay.

28

> Thou sawest till that a stone was cut out without hands, which smote the image upon his feet that were of iron and clay, and brake them to pieces.
>
> Daniel 2:31-34

Then Daniel gave the king the interpretation. God revealed through Daniel that the great metallic colossus foretold the future of mankind.

The metallic man revealed four great prophetic world empires — the entire period of Gentile supremacy in the world — until the end of time.

Gold — Babylonian Empire

> Thou, O king, art a king of kings; for the God of heaven hath given thee a kingdom, power, and strength, and glory. And wheresoever the children of men dwell, the beasts of the field and the fowls of the heaven hath he given into thine hand, and hath made thee ruler over them all. Thou art this head of gold.
>
> Daniel 2:37,38

The golden empire of the centuries was Babylon (Iraq) — none ever rose such as it. Babylon fell to the Persians (Iran) in 539 B.C.

Silver — Medo-Persian Empire

> After thee shall arise another kingdom inferior to thee . . . .
>
> Daniel 2:39

Our first prophetic picture of Iran — shoulders, arms, and chest of silver. The empire indeed had two arms — the Medes and the Persians. They were together, members of the same family. The Persians superseded the Medes and dominated the kingdom.

Brass — Grecian Empire

> . . . and another third kingdom of brass, which shall bear rule over all the earth.
>
> Daniel 2:39

This kingdom began with Alexander the Great and was later controlled by four army generals. In 334 B.C. Alexander set about liberating Greece from Persian control and launching the sweeping campaign which resulted in a new empire.

Iron (Clay and Iron) — Roman Empire

And the fourth kingdom shall be strong as iron.
Daniel 2:40

The Roman empire arose two hundred years before Christ. It was seen first divided into two — the legs — fulfilled in the Eastern and Western Roman empires. Then it was seen divided into ten — the toes (the feet and toes were clay and iron) — this is the federation of nations under one head, the Antichrist, which exists at the end of the present age.

Second Prophetic Picture of Iraq/Iran: The Bear

King Nebuchadnezzar's vision of the metallic man gave the imposing outward glory of the destiny of empires. God revealed their natures in a vision given to Daniel forty-eight years later.

In the first year of Belshazzar king of Babylon Daniel had a dream and visions of his head upon his bed . . . Daniel spake and said, I saw in my vision by night, and behold, the four winds of the heaven strove upon the great sea.
Daniel 7:1,2

This reveals the movement of strength and might upon multitudes of people. In God's Word "the sea" is always multitudes of people. Daniel saw the furious empires of the world moving like tempestuous winds upon a stormy sea.

And four great beasts came up from the sea (again the sea of people), **diverse one from another** (v. 3). Every empire in history has been different from all others.

The first was like a lion, and had eagle's wings ... (v. 4). This kingdom is the same as the golden head. It is now described as a lion. As gold is the finest of metals, so the lion is the strongest of beasts. Babylon was a much greater nation than many modern people realize. The lion had eagle's wings. This signifies the speed in which it moved to conquer the world and carry out its own wishes. Great strength and velocity symbolized Babylon.

Our special interest in this book is the second empire.

> **And behold another beast, a second, like to a bear,and it raised up itself on one side, and it had three ribs in the mouth of it between the teeth of it: and they said thus unto it, Arise, devour much flesh.**
>
> **Verse 5**

In Daniel's vision Persia was a bear.

The Medes and the Persians were one army together — but Persia raised itself up on one side and destroyed the Medes. Thus it became solely the Persian empire.

The three ribs in the bear's mouth signify three major nations it had conquered — Media, Lydia, and Babylon. All were conquered by Persia. Persia boasted that she ruled 127 provinces from India to Egypt.

All the great empires were ruthless and killed many. "Much flesh devoured" speaks of the terrible violence and quick destruction exacted upon this

31

empire's enemies. The bear is a vicious predator, a killer. In like manner, Persia was a devourer of nations.

> After his I beheld, and lo another, like a leopard, which had upon the back of it four wings of a foul; the beast had also four heads; and dominion was given to it.
>
> **Verse 6**

The Grecian empire was known for its great speed, for its hiding, and for its killing. God likened it unto a leopard with four wings and four heads.

> After this I saw in the night visions, and behold a fourth beast, dreadful and terrible, and strong exceedingly; and it had great iron teeth; it devoured and brake in pieces, and stamped the residue with the feet of it; and it was diverse from all the beasts that were before it; and it had ten horns.
>
> **Verse 7**

The fourth beast was unlike any other beast. It was the Roman empire. In the end it was to have ten horns, representing ten nations, and a little horn which ultimately produces the Antichrist who will stand up before Christ and fight against him at the end of time.

Third Prophetic Picture
of Iraq/Iran: Ram

Two years after the vision recorded in Daniel chapter 7, the Lord gave Daniel a further vision of empires. This vision came to him in the third year of Belshazzar (553 B.C.).

Daniel says something very strange as he begins to relate it:

> I saw in a vision; and it came to pass, when I saw, that I saw at Shushan in the palace, which is in the

**province of Elam; and I saw in a vision, and I was
by the river of Ulai.**

Daniel 8:2

We already know the province of Elam becomes
Persia and then Iraq/Iran. Shushan is its Persian capital
and the structure of the royal palace. The royal city was
known as "Shushan the palace." The business and
residential area was known as "Shushan the city."
Daniel saw that world power was to be transferred to
the kingdom of Persia. This would be fulfilled fourteen
years later in 539 B.C.

**Then I lifted up mine eyes, and saw, and,
behold, there stood before the river a ram which had
two horns; and the two horns were high; but one was
higher than the other, and the higher came up last.**

Verse 3

God gave Daniel the interpretation of the ram in
verse 20: **The ram which thou sawest having two horns
are the kings of Media and Persia.**

The two horns represent the twin nations of the
Medes and the Persians in the beginning. Then one
horn lifted itself up higher than the other and the
Persians destroyed the Medes and became sole rulers
of the empire.

**I saw the ram pushing westward, and northward,
and southward . . . .**

Verse 4

The ram's thrust of power was westward toward
Israel and the Mediterranean Sea, northward toward
Russia and Turkey, and southward toward Africa.
Persia boasted that all existing armies were defeated
and her rule was over one hundred twenty-seven
provinces with a prince ruling each province.

Daniel also saw the fall of the Persian empire. He tells of a great "he goat" coming from the west (v. 5). Greece is in the west. The he goat did not touch the ground. He moved with such velocity and power and speed, he ran into the ram which was Persia — smote him, broke his horns, cast him to the ground and stomped upon him.

Therefore the he goat waxed very great . . . .
Verse 8

The Grecian empire began to rule the world.
. . . and when he was strong, the great horn was broken; and for it came up four notable ones toward the four winds of heaven.
Verse 8

Alexander the Great died at a very young age. Four generals ruled, dividing his kingdom.

History Before It Happens

These prophesies by the prophet Daniel became an accurate record of history which was to come.

One of the proofs that God is God is that many years before these empires came into power, God through his servants revealed the empires' likeness, their strength, their rise and their fall, and the one that would succeed them — even unto the last empire which has to do with the Stone which was cut without hands out of the mountain. We will discuss more about this later.

6
Iraq/Iran —
Rebuilding the Walls
of Israel

It is remarkable that we can follow Noah's grandson, Elam, through the pages of history until his tribe becomes a mighty empire — an empire which blessed the work of God.

The Babylonian empire had conquered Israel, destroying its capital city, Jerusalem — its walls, its gates, its Temple. The Babylonian empire robbed the Temple of its treasures and carried them away to Babylon.

The Persian empire returned the captives to their homeland and helped them rebuild their walls, their gates, and their Temple, giving them money and provisions to do so. They returned the vessels of the House of the Lord which Nebuchadnezzar had brought to Babylon. (Ezra 1:7-11).

The Books of Ezra, Nehemiah, Esther, Isaiah, Jeremiah, Haggai, Zechariah, and Malachi testify to this. They tell the story of the Persian empire as related to the people through whom God would bring a Savior to the world. They prophesy relating to Iraq/Iran and its destiny.

Cyrus, king of Persia, founded the Medo-Persian empire. He is the king who returned the Jews to Judea.

Ezra chapter 1 tells his story and declares that it was the Lord who stirred him up to do so.

> Now in the first year of Cyrus king of Persia, that the word of the Lord by the mouth of Jeremiah might be fulfilled, the Lord stirred up the spirit of Cyrus king of Persia, that he make a proclamation throughout all his kingdom, and put it also in writing, saying, Thus saith Cyrus king of Persia, the Lord God of heaven hath given me all the kingdoms of the earth; and he hath charged me to build him an house at Jerusalem, which is in Judah.
>
> Ezra 1:1,2

It is fascinating that the prophet Isaiah had foretold this — even naming the king — seventy-six years before. (Is. 44:28; 45:1,13.)

The son of Cyrus, Cambyses, became emperor of Persia at his father's death. He went forth to conquer Egypt and was fantastically successful in putting down rebellion in Egypt. But on his journey home he died.

An imposter named Pseudo Smerdis grabbed the throne for the emperor was out of the country when he died. He ruled Persia six months before being killed by Darius.

King Darius, after taking the throne, defeated nine kings in nineteen battles. He brought Persia to an unquestionable place of supremacy in the world, putting down all rebellion in the world against it.

The Temple Rebuilt

During the reign of Darius, Jerusalem was a scene of activity between 520 and 515 B.C., as the Temple was rebuilt under the prophetic leadership of Haggai and Zechariah.

The Walls Go Up

Nehemiah, a Jew, was cupbearer to the famous Persian king, Artaxerxes. In Nehemiah 1:4 we observe this man in high position to be a man of prayer. His determination was so strong he prayed for four months before appearing before the king to present his cause.

Because of his acceptance by the Persian king, he was commissioned to go to Jerusalem and rebuild the walls and the gates.

The emperor provided Nehemiah with finances and letters to all the governors of the provinces and gave him protection.

The People May Return

Ezra (also a leader of Israel) was greatly respected and found favor with Artaxerxes. So much so that the king made this decree:

> **I make a decree, that all they of the people of Israel, and of his priests and Levites, in my realm, which are minded of their own freewill to go up to Jerusalem, go with thee.**
>
> **Ezra 7:13**

This was decreed in 457 B.C.

Iraq/Iran had a very vital part in the rebirth of Israel. What the empire of Babylon had destroyed, the empire of Persia had rebuilt.

When Iraq/Iran gave sympathy to the Jews and helped them to rebuild, it played a part in the plan of God. For it was through these Jews that a way was being prepared for the eternal King, Jesus, to come.

7

Preventing
a First "Great Holocaust"

It is amazing how God keeps putting His finger into politics.

He has always had a witness in every empire. When Egypt was the greatest country in the world, Joseph was right there bossing the thing. When Babylon was at the zenith of its power, Daniel was there giving the forecast and the truth for the land. And at the peak of the Persian empire, a Jewish queen came to the throne.

Ahasuerus, son of Darius, had succeeded his father to the throne. This Ahasuerus, or Xerxes, was a militant emperor. He maintained the scope and splendor of the Persian empire and was successful in keeping his more restless subjects under control.

He ruled from India even unto Ethiopia over one hundred twenty-seven provinces (Esth. 1:1). This is the vastness of the Persian empire.

Under Ahasuerus, an amazing page of history took place in "Shushan the palace" — capital city of the world. All nations brought their gold and silver to this city of world dictatorship. This city is located one hundred fifty miles north of the Persian Gulf east of the Tigris River. The Persians called it Sush then (Sushan is Hebrew) — today it is called Shush.

It was in this city that Queen Esther's divine destiny preserved a nation.

"Shushan the palace" was a city within the city — a royal capital. The story begins with a remarkably long feast that took place there.

> **In the third year of his reign, he (Ahasuerus) made a feast unto all his princes and his servants; the power of Persia and Media, the nobles and princes of the provinces being before him: When he shewed the riches of his glorious kingdom and the honour of his excellent majesty many days, even an hundred and fourscore days.**
>
> **Esther 1:3,4**

How would you like to attend a feast that lasted six months? When that feast was over, he had another one.

> **And when these days were expired, the king made a feast unto all the people that were present in Shushan the palace, both unto great and small, seven days, in the court of the garden of the king's palace.**
>
> **Verse 5**

> Those garden courts were fabulously decorated (v. 6). **And they gave them drink in vessels of gold, (the vessels being diverse one from another,) and royal wine in abundance . . . .**
>
> **Esther 1:7**

Everyone had a cup made of gold. Several thousand people and no two cups were alike!.

These Persians were exceedingly rich.

It is a sad story, but after the feast and the drunken mess, the king asked Queen Vashti to come forward and show her flesh. She would not. So he banished her.

A search went forth throughout all the provinces for all the fair young virgins to be brought unto Shushan the palace to the house of the women. The maiden who pleased the king would be queen instead of Vashti.

In Shushan the palace there was a certain Jew, Mordecai. He was a great man for he sat in the gate of the capital. This meant he had to do with the discourses of the government. This is where they gave justice and answered the problems of the people.

Mordecai had brought up his uncle's orphaned daughter, Hadassah, that is, Esther. She was fair of form and beautiful.

It came to pass that Esther was chosen by the king as the most beautiful maiden and she became queen of the Persian empire.

Special Delivery

In the Book of Nehemiah it is written that God gave his people **saviors, who saved them out of the hand of their enemies** (Neh. 9:27).

In the reign of Esther we have one of these special deliveries. It is one of the most fascinating accounts in history.

A man named Haman — a Hitler of his day — who was a Persian prince and stood next to the emperor, planned the total annihilation of the people of Israel.

The king had promoted Haman and advanced him above all the princes. When Haman rode through the streets he asked that everyone in the king's gate bow before him.

One man at the gate would not bow. That was the Jew Mordecai.

Haman was furious. He asked who the man was and why he would not bow.

They told him it was Mordecai, and that he was a Jew.

So Haman said, "I will destroy all Jews."

He gathered information about the Jews and went before the king. The crux of the matter was this. Haman said, "I want to destroy those people called the Jews. I will pay for it myself." He promised $20 million of his personal funds to finance the job.

What he did not know was, Queen Esther was a Jewess. Esther had not yet revealed her lineage.

When Mordecai learned of Haman's plan to destroy all the Jews in all one hundred twenty-seven provinces, he rushed word to Esther charging her that **she should go in unto the king, to make supplication unto him, and to make request before him for her people** (Esth. 4:8).

The law of the land was that if anyone, man or woman, should come unto the king who was not called, they would be put to death — unless the king held out his golden sceptre that the person should live.

Esther had not been called to come unto the king for 30 days.

Mordecai sent these powerful words to Esther, **Who knoweth whether thou art come to the kingdom for such a time as this?** (Esth. 4:14).

Queen Esther took her life into her hands and went before the king.

And it was so, when the king saw Esther the queen standing in the court, that she obtained favour in his sight; and the king held out to Esther the golden sceptre that was in his hand. So Esther drew near, and touched the top of the sceptre.

Esther 5:2

Esther found favor with the Persian, or Iranian, shah and delivered the people of God.

Haman died for his sins. He was hung on the gallows he had prepared for Mordecai.

The Jews were preserved.

And the empire got to know of the true and living God.

Immortal Peace Day Related to Iraq/Iran

At the death of Haman and the salvation of the Jews a great feast was celebrated. (Esth. 9:17.) It was called the Feast of Purim. To this day it is celebrated to Jews all over the world during the first part of February.

I have personally seen the Israeli children play and march through the streets of Israel on this festive day. The mothers bake small cakes in the shape of a triangle which they give to various people on this special peace day. It is a day of rejoicing.

8

The Unmistakable Link
to the Birth of Christ

It is most remarkable how certain nations became Biblically oriented where the lineage of the nation can be traced similarly to the lineage of a family.

It is also a lesson to learn that when God becomes involved with a person or a nation they owe certain allegiances to Him.

Also, when light comes across our pathway, we must live up to that light or darkness comes into our lives or into our nation. We see that the darkness came into the present nations of Iraq/Iran, which in 1935 were known as Persia, a name which took the nation back twenty-five hundred years to the time it was called Elam. This nation has had many opportunities to love God and to serve God — and it still has opportunities today.

As Iraq/Iran have been involved in Bible history from the time of Noah, they will continue to be a part of Bible prophecy until the Kingdom of Christ is fulfilled.

Wise Men from Iraq/Iran

Now when Jesus was born in Bethlehem of Judaea in the days of Herod the king, behold, there came wise men from the east to Jerusalem, Saying,

> **Where is he that is born King of the Jews? for we have
> seen his star in the east, and are come to worship him.**
> **Matthew 2:1,2**

This is one of the most amazing stories in the Bible. It certainly has to do with the supernatural.

How could they know a king was to be born?

How could they know he was to be king of the Jews?

How could they be interested in a Jewish king?

Why was it a star they followed?

Possibly these men were acquainted with the Torah of the writings of Moses. Maybe they knew Numbers 24:17, . . . **there shall come a Star out of Jacob, and a Sceptre shall rise out of Israel . . . .** If they knew prophecy and loved God, they would be searching the heavens for such a star. Certainly they had to be guided supernaturally in order to arrive at this place at this specific time in history.

Persian history relates that these men came from their area, from Elam. It says they were trained in medicine, natural sciences, and astronomy. Today three Iranian cities make claims that the kings mentioned in Matthew were from their city. These are Savaha, Mahadam, and Razyach.

There are remarkable situations in this story.

One is that they were willing to follow a star in the heavens that was guiding them — whatever that star was.

It is also remarkable that they were willing to do worship and humble themselves before a child. They expressly said they had come to worship Him.

It is interesting to see that Joseph and Mary were no longer in a barn or cow stable. They were in a house when they were found.

> **And when they were come into the house, they saw the young child with Mary his mother, and fell down, and worshipped him; and when they had opened their treasures, they presented unto him gifts; gold, and frankincense, and myrrh.**
>
> **Matthew 2:11**

It is interesting that the commodities in the open market where money could easily be obtained were gold, frankincense, and myrrh. They opened their treasures and presented these three gifts to Jesus.

This was adequate for support for a great length of time. It could take Mary and Joseph and the Child to Egypt. They could live there comfortably. And they could return to their own home safely.

God could have arranged many other things to help the Lord Jesus to go into Egypt for protection against King Herod who finally destroyed the boy babies two years old and younger in Bethlehem. For sure, there were rich people about who could have supplied funds for their escape.

Why would the Lord reach back to the place He had brought Abraham from in the beginning and bring forth these people across the burning deserts to this area? Probably we will not understand the full story until we are in heaven.

Certainly, it links Iraq/Iran with the Bible story in a most intrinsic way. It reveals that God has an interest in the people of that area. It reveals that the people are willing to find and follow divine revelation. It reveals that they were willing to meet a need which was urgent at that time.

It binds Iraq/Iran forever with the birth of the Savior of the world. The story of the wise men guarantees that the true story of the Savior of the world was told in the Persian land. For those wise men would not have left Bethlehem until Mary had told all — until Joseph had told all — until the Scriptures from Isaiah were clearly explained how a virgin would conceive and bear a child.

9
Charter Members
of the Christian Church

When the Son of God was born on planet earth, He came with direct and explicit instructions to save this planet form its sins. This was brought about through the Jewish nation.

Yet though Christ was born into a Jewish family, it was the Iraqis and Iranians who came and brought the money to take Christ and His family to safety and to support them during their moment of need.

The next great event in history after Christ ascended to heaven was the birth of the Christian church. Could it be possible that these people of Iraq/Iran, who were connected with the birth of the Savior, could also be involved in any way with the birth of the Christian Church?

Possibly the most revolutionary day in history was the day the Church was born. Jesus had already said the gates of hell could not prevail against it! (Matt. 16:18.)

Jesus has already divided humanity into two sections — they that believe and they that believe not.

Now a mighty force — the Church — came into being! The story is told in Acts chapter 2:

> **And when the day of Pentecost was fully come, they were all with one accord in one place. And suddenly there came a sound from heaven as of a rushing mighty wind, and it filled all the house where they were sitting. And there appeared unto them cloven tongues like as of fire, and it sat upon each of them. And they were all filled with the Holy Ghost, and began to speak with other tongues, as the Spirit gave them utterance.**
>
> **Verses 1-4**

The day had fully come. The Roman roads were ready for them to travel upon. The ships of the world were ready to carry them across its waves. The arsenals of the Roman empire were ready to protect travelers as they journeyed from continent to continent, from nation to nation. The world was ready. God was ready.

Most intensely interesting is who was there the day the Church was born.

At the initial infilling, there were one hundred twenty people in an upper room in a private home. Mary, the mother of Jesus, was there. She belonged to the royal family. The eleven disciples and apostles, who had been with Him from the beginning and were the foundation stones of the Christian Church, were there. A few others are identified. And beyond this, there were more than 100 whose names or addresses we do not know, but they were among those who made it possible for the Church to be born.

After receiving the Holy Spirit, this ecstatic group flowed out of the Upper Room into the Temple area where there was room for everybody. There they found many openhearted people ready to hear.

> **And there were dwelling at Jerusalem Jews, devout men, out of every nation under heaven.**
>
> **Verse 5**

How remarkable that Jews and converts to Judaism from throughout the world were in the Temple area to worship God at this great feast of Pentecost on the day the Church was born!

Now when this was noised abroad, the multitude came together, and were confounded, because that every man heard them speak in his own language.
Verse 6

This miracle simply astounded them. They were amazed. They marvelled, saying one to another, **Behold, are not all these which speak Galilaeans? And how hear we every man in our own tongue, wherein we were born? Parthian, and Medes, and Elamites . . .**

(vv. 7-9).

Other nations were named, but we will identify these three named first. The Parthians were from the area called Pars, also called Fars, which is in southern Iraq/Iran. The Medes were located in central Iraq/Iran. The Elamites were from southwestern Iraq/Iran and the capital city of Shushan.

The Iranians were there the day the Church was born!

And they went back home and began to plant the Church in their own area. The Church was planted in Persia. Tradition says that Andrew lived in that area — that Bartholomew was a missionary to Armenia — that Thomas labored in Parthia — and that Jude preached and died in Persia. They had living Apostles.

But Iraq/Iran is not Christian today; it is Moslem. Why?

10
Jihad: The Holy War of Islam

Webster's New World Dictionary defines *Jihad:* ''A war by Moslems against unbelievers or enemies of Islam, carried out as a religious duty.''

Beyond any doubt, among the shifting sands of the Arabian Peninsula, world destiny is being formed. It is very difficult for America to comprehend the vast importance of what is happening in the Middle East at this time.

Iraq/Iran has made itself the center of Jihad. Its total population is in a frenzy. Suddenly, again emerges the Persian empire.

America's carnal Christians do not realize that the battles of our time are spiritual. In the whole vast world today, the true issues are spiritual.

To understand Jihad one must know certain things about Islam. To know those things about Islam, one must know certain things about Mohammed and his times.

The World of Mohammed

When Mohammed came on the scene of human activity, the power of Persia was devastated and gone; a bad memory. The Grecian empire had sunk into decay and was no longer a world power. Even the Roman empire lay at its lowest level in dust and defeat.

The Dark Ages had settled over the Western world. The Bible was locked in the cloistered recesses of monasteries away from the common people. There were no other books. And only 15 percent of the population could read or write.

After the birth of the Christian Church, the Fertile Crescent enjoyed a great thrust of spiritual growth and of the power of God. Many churches were formed. And the Church grew in a wonderful and delightful way. But during the centuries from the first century to the sixth, the Church lost its emphasis, its zeal, its fervor. It ceased to grow either materially or spiritually.

The world was ripe for a revolutionary religion such as Islam to be born. And from the dusty wastes of Arabia, the people were ready for a prophet, good or bad.

So often when we are not positive to produce the person God wants to lead and guide, the devil will give counterfeits. So many times, the one that God wants is not available because people are not ready for such a one.

Mohammed was born in 570 A.D. in the city of Mecca, thirty years before the end of the sixth century. He died in 632 A.D. at sixty-two years of age.

The story of Mohammed is that of a child of misfortune. His father died two months before his birth. His mother died when he was six. He was reared by his grandfather, who died later, and then his uncle, Abu Talib.

Abu was a businessman and a trader. His merchant caravans followed the Fertile Crescent from

Iran to Egypt. Mohammed greatly enjoyed following these caravans with his uncle and his nephew, Ali.

At the age of twenty-five, Mohammed was a chief camel driver working for Khadija, a wealthy Jewish widow. Three years later, he married her though she was some twenty years older than he was.

Owning a caravan was like owning a railroad or an airline today. He got to know personally far away lands such as Syria, Palestine, and Egypt. He had much time to visit, to talk, to listen about religion and about philosophy.

For with his newly gained wealth and prestige, Mohammed pursued his consuming desire. He was constantly seeking for something that would satisfy his inner man. He was a thirsting man. Oh, if only someone could have met him and have given him the real truth!

He knew the Jews and Christians of his day.

The Jews had ample opportunity to win young Mohammed to the Jewish faith, to the true God, to the Ten Commandments. Though the contacts were many, this was not done. Possibly the Jewish leaders did not feel that this youth would mean much to the world and they paid no attention to him.

The Christians also had many contacts with him. He probably sat in many of their services and listened to them. It could be that the inconsistency of their business practices and lives could not convince him to follow their religion.

He did not see a spirit or a power in either the Jews or the Christians to convince him. But his writings show that he was influenced by them. He calls

Abraham his father like the Jews call him their father. The Koran, the sacred book of Islam, includes a strange story of Mary and the birth of Jesus.

He often retired to a cave to meditate upon religion. One day he had a vision which changed his destiny. He decided he was a prophet sent from Allah. He considered himself one of six great prophets sent from Allah. He called Adam a prophet, which he was not. He called Noah a prophet, which he was. He called Abraham a prophet, Moses a prophet, and Jesus a prophet. Of himself he said, "I am the last of the great prophets."

It is possible to stay alone and fabricate your own ideas until you get way out into desolation spiritually, thinking you are right. People living today have themselves way out in some corner, into cults and error.

The Word of God is Truth! And we have had it from the beginning of time. Paul said that even if an angel from heaven preaches any other gospel, we are not to accept it. (Gal. 1:8.)

For after all, Satan himself can appear as an angel of light, as can his ministers. (2 Cor. 11:14.)

We cannot accept any private revelations. The revelation God gave is in the Bible. Eternal Life is in the Bible.

Mohammed's Revelations

Mohammed heard voices. They came to him, not once or twice, but over a period of twenty-three years. He claimed the angel Gabriel dictated the Koran to him word by word.

The Koran, according to Mohammed, annuls the Bible. He declared that the Bible was corrupted by both Jews and Christians and not reliable.

Mohammed said in the Koran that Gabriel transmitted Islam's teachings undefiled, unmatched, and uncreated. He said they existed in heaven from the beginning.

The Koran has 114 Suras, or chapters, and contains 77,639 words.

In the Sura, XCVIII:5-7, Mohammed taught that Christians, Jews, and idolaters are the worst of all created beings — and that Moslem believers are the best of all created beings.

In the Sura IV:14,29; IV:84,101,104, Mohammed taught that love is not as important as obedience or submission.

The Koran strictly teaches its followers to love their own believers — but not disbelievers. It encourages Moslems to wage a war (Jihad) against non-Moslems in the name of Islam.

To kill a non-Moslem is justifiable. What is not permitted is to kill a believer, unless by mistake, in which case blood money must be paid to the victim's family.

Mohammed made polygamy a way of life. He gave Moslems permission to have four wives, although he himself had ten wives. He said this was through special permission from Allah.

Incidentally, after Khadijah died, within a year Mohammed married three more wives. One had been the wife of his adopted son. Another was a Jewish woman. The third was a Coptic Christian. Mohammed certainly must have heard the Old and New Testament stories from these women. His Koran contains Bible stories terribly twisted.

Mohammedanism teaches that Satan does not affect a man's relationship with Allah. Neither does the Adamic nature of the human transmit sin to its offspring. Islam teaches that man is born sinless, that man has a tendency to sin; however, he has the ability to rise above his sins.

It is not man's relationship with God as much as it is the believer's relationship with other believers that is of great significance.

Bloodshed: Way to Sell a New Religion

The first person Mohammed convinced of his new religion was his wife, Khadijah. His nephew, Ali, was the second. Many Moslems today are named after this Ali who became a strong supporter of Mohammed and his ideas and was one of the first leaders of the new religion.

Mohammed had a difficult time teaching his new religion. He was persecuted and driven from his native Mecca to Medina. His flight is called "Hegira." He gathered his faithful around him and taught them that the only way to win the world to Allah was by force, with the sword.

The forceful overthrow of the government of Medina came in 622 A.D., the same year he arrived. The city was converted to Islam — except for some Jews and a few Christians — and Mohammed became its ruler as well as its religious high priest.

The former camel driver turned prophet, priest, ruler, lawgiver, and judge, also became commander-in-chief of Jihad's first armed forces. He attacked Mecca, defeated its army, destroyed its idols, and established the new religion of Islam.

Medina and Mecca, where it all started, are the most holy places of the confederation. As the Jews taught Mohammed to face Jerusalem to pray, he taught his followers to face Mecca to pray.

At the time of his death, Mohammed had united almost all Arabia politically and religiously under Moslem control. And he had turned his thoughts toward Persia and the world.

After his death, the enthusiasm of Islam began to rise in fanatical fury. Those near him were determined to carry on his cause. They captured area after area and planted the Crescent and the new religion of Islam.

Islam's leaders were fierce and uncompromising. To disobey them was to die.

In less than twenty-five years, Mohammed's followers had captured Persia, Syria, Palestine, and Egypt.

In less than seventy-five years, they had taken North Africa and had entered Europe through Spain. It was only by a miracle of God that Charles Martel defeated the Moslems at the Battle of Tours in 732 A.D. and stopped the progress of Islam in Europe.

Islam had become the dominant power of the Mediterranean world. Its realm of influence stretched from the Atlantic Ocean to the borders of China, encompassing all the great empires of past history.

During the seventh and eighth centuries, Islam moved westward into Central Asia. Irresistibly, century after century, it gained converts until most of Northern India had fallen before its sword. In the fifteenth and sixteenth centuries, Islam moved toward the Far East into Java, Sumatra, and many islands, including the Philippines.

All of the bloodshed was justifiable in the name of Jihad. One of Islam's greatest leaders was Abu Bekr, who immediately followed Mohammed into leadership. He wrote to cities and countries of Arabia to become subservient to the new religion. He sent his followers into Syria to take out of the hands of the infidels the powers of state and religion. He told them, "And I would have you know that fighting for religion is an act of obedience to Allah."

The first Syrian city he conquered was Bosra. A man named Romanus was the leader of this city. The invaders caused him to say publicly these words, "I deny Him that was crucified, and whosoever worships Him. I choose God for my Lord, Islam for my faith, Mecca for my temple, the Moslems for my brethren, and Mohammed for my prophet." (*The History of Nations*, by Lodge, page 418.)

Islam and Iraq/Iran

When the Islamic religion invaded Iraq/Iran, possibly the hardest persecuted were the Zoroastrians. When Islam became the State religion, its leaders slowly persecuted the Christians and other dissenters. It assessed them extra taxes. It forbade Christians to make converts. It refused Christians the permission to display the Cross at all. Persecution varied by the provinces and also by the rulers over them.

In the early history of Iraq/Iran, the Church had prospered under kings such as Sassiens from 224 A.D. to 642 A.D. The city of Shush was the center of Christianity. But with the coming of Islam, the Church was overwhelmed. By the time Genghis Khan, the Mongol monarch, marched across Iraq/Iran in the middle 1200s, the Church was almost eliminated. The remnant fled to the mountains in western Iraq/Iran. And the Church never knew strength again in that land.

Christianity Today in Iraq/Iran

The largest professing group of Christians in Iraq/Iran are the Armenians, possibly one hundred sixty thousand strong. These Armenians date back to the first century. They are a closely knit people who mostly intermarry. The book, *Christians in Persia*, states that in the year 1624 Shah Abbas passed a law that any Christian who became a Moslem could claim the property of any of his relatives back to at least four generations. It was said that possibly fifty thousand Christians renounced their faith in order to get property. Very few of these were Armenians.

Holy Places: Price of Non-Evangelism

Maybe the strongest thing we could say in this book is that the Jews had ample time and place to win Mohammed to their religion. In this, they failed.

What they did not know was that the day would come when a Moslem mosque, the Mosque of Omar, would be erected in Jerusalem near the very site of

Solomon's Temple. Rather than the prayers of the Jews being heard in that place, there would be prayers to Allah.

To the Jews, one of the most sacred spots on the earth is Hebron where Abraham lived, where the angels talked to him at his front door, and the cave of Machpelah where he is buried. Five patriarchs are buried in the cave at Hebron. But rather than its being a Jewish place of reverence, respect, and prayer, it has a Moslem mosque over it. Islamic prayers are screamed from the minaret towers five times a day.

What a tremendous reminder that if we do not win sinners to Christ, they will turn and destroy us. I have so often wondered what a different world we would have if some Christian in Austria had won Adolf Hitler to the Lord Jesus Christ. It could have saved 50 million people from destruction by the war! When we do not evangelize, we suffer the consequences of it. Any person you refuse to win to Christ can become your adversary.

Christians, too, had ample opportunity to win Mohammed. He met many of them in his travels across the Fertile Crescent passing through Syria and Palestine into Egypt. He must have known much about Christianity. He saw its large churches, met its dignitaries, yet no one converted him.

One result is that possibly the most sacred place on earth for the Christians — the top of Mount Calvary — is a Moslem cemetery.

Few Christians ever walk on that mountain. Steel gates, a big chain, and a lock keep them out. I have been up there several times, especially where I lived in Israel. I always gave the porter a gift, but even then there is a reluctance to admit an "infidel" to walk around those Moslem graves on Mount Calvary.

As one looks up at the face of Golgotha (meaning skull) and sees the indentations in the side of the rock which must have given it its name, immediately below he sees an Arab bus station.

From early morning to late evening animals cry as they are carried in and out, all kinds of freight is continuously handled, busses toot their horns, people scream and yell in front of Calvary making it one of the most active spots of humanity I have seen — and all this within ten feet of Golgotha where the Son of God gave His life to save the entire human race.

This bus station was not built in 1950, when I first began visiting the Holy Land. I wrote a letter to the mayor of Jerusalem, whom I knew when we lived there, asking him if it could be moved. He answered that the Moslem population would never permit such a thing.

What a price Christendom paid for not evangelizing everyone, everywhere with the Gospel of the Lord Jesus Christ! Today the Moslem religion has over one billion followers.

The most populous Moslem nation in the world is Indonesia with over 100 million Moslems. Africa has 225 million, Europe has 20 million, and the United States has a possible two million Moslems. Russia has 54 million Moslems within its borders. Moslems are growing at the rate of 25 million per year. Christianity sees only 1,000 born again Moslems in a year.

World Dominance

A Moslem leader recently said, "Unless we win London to Islam, we will fail to win the whole of the Western world."

The whole of the Western world is the ambition of the Moslem world.

In London there are some six hundred thousand Moslems today. They have 300 mosques scattered over the city. The Central Mosque and Islamic Cultural Center was built in Regents Park in London at a cost of $7.5 million.

Is it possible that the nations of the West have not yet begun to realize the confrontation that is before them? For Jihad is the religious "duty" of the world's Moslems.

11

The Crusades of Failure

Possibly the greatest time of slaughter during the conflict between the Crescent and the Cross was during the crusades when Christians of Europe undertook military expeditions to recover the Holy Land from the Moslems.

They began in 1096 A.D. when Peter the Hermit moved possibly six million people in Europe into a fury, begging them to regain the holy places in Palestine for the Christians.

He personally led a crusade of men — who history relates were unprepared in training and arms, neither did they understand the difficulties and dangers of their conflict. Most perished enroute from exposure, hunger, disease, and war.

A decisive battle was the famous battle at the Horns of Hattin fought in 1187 A.D. The Crusaders had passed from the Mediterranean to Nazareth where they settled. Their strategy was to go over the Galilean hills to the Sea of Galilee and engage the Moslem sultan, Saladin, and his forces in conflict.

King Guy of England had 20,000 soldiers and 120 knights. What he did not realize was, the Moslems had an army of 80,000 awaiting him. Many died in the bloody slaughter that ensued.

The crusades continued from the end of the eleventh century until the end of the thirteenth century. Millions suffered and died on both sides. Both sides claimed Abraham as their father and that they believed in the one true God.

It is one of the darkest pictures of human history.

12
Fanning the Flames of War

Upon the entry of Islam into the world in the sixth century, the deserts rang out with a new cry: "Jihad! Holy War!"

This new religion on the world's scene would stand up angrily before the old religions. It would demand its place in the forum of religions.

It would differ greatly from Buddhism, already 1,000 years old. There could be no idols or multiplicity of gods. In fact, there could be only the one God as the Judeo-Christian religions believed.

This oft-repeated tenet of the Moslem faith makes it clear: there is no god but Allah; Mohammed is his prophet.

This newest of religions would bring a new world. It would use the sword to convert tribes, nations and empires to Islam.

The hot sands of Arabia would become bloody sands of religious fanaticism. Synagogues of the Jews and churches of the Christians would be turned into Mosques.

Today, in the twentieth century, the backbones of Western statesmen are trembling as persistent and prophetic voices are heard coming from the burning sands of ancient Persia, Babylon, Elam, Ur and Shushan.

The voices are crying to the Moslem world, "We want Jihad! We want Holy War!"

Iraq/Iran and Jihad

The crisis in the nation of Iran where sixty-three hostages were taken from the American Embassy in Tehran (ten were later released) by militants and radicals was not a political maneuver. It was not an accidental situation.

It was spiritual! It is prophetical!

Modern Iran with its population of 35 million people and its relation with ancient Persia has a remarkable relationship to prophetic destiny — much of which remains to be fulfilled.

Shah Mohammad Reza Pahlavi, like Esther's husband before him, knew how to hold sumptuous festivities. In 1971, he held a wild $100 million celebration to commemorate 2,500 years of recorded history. This man's father had changed the name from Persia to Iran in 1935.

However, as we have seen, the true story of Iraq/Iran and the Middle East actually dates back 4,000 years. The people of that area can measure their times from Noah's Ark to the Antichrist.

Not many nations have survived such millennia. Iran and Iraq went through the terror of the Tower of Babel when in one night all the languages and dialects of the world were created by God. They were a people in the days of Peleg when God divided the continents, sub-continents, islands, and scattered the seas.

It is easy to measure the time of Iran's and Iraq's lineage from Noah's son, Elam.

The Bible records ten generations from Noah to Abraham. (Gen. 11.) Matthew 1:17 specifically states that from Abraham to David was 14 generations — from David to Babylon was 14 generations — and from Babylon to Christ was 14 generations. This totals 52 generations. If a generation is 40 years, as the Bible says, this equals 2,080 years.

And, of course, today's calendar counts time from Christ until now in a reasonably close proximity. Therefore, the roots of Iran and Iraq can be traced 4,000 years.

We have also traced the religious roots of Iran and Iraq and have seen how Islam became the principle ruling religion of this Moslem state.

A House Divided

It should be realized not all Arabs are Moslems. Many evangelical Arabs belong to Baptist, Methodist, Presbyterian, and Full Gospel churches.

The Coptic Church is one of the oldest churches in the world, dating back before the birth of Islam.

We have already mentioned the American Arabs who have held fast to their Christian beliefs through many centuries of persecutions.

Druids are scattered throughout the Arab world, but they are not Moslems.

Turkey has a large number of Kurds as do Iran and Iraq.

The Arabs who are Moslems are divided into a number of sects.

The Summa, also know as Sunni, make up approximately 90 percent of all Moslems. This largest group is more conservative.

The Shiites compose only about ten percent of the Moslem religion. They are the more militant.

The Shiites believe that the successors of Mohammed by heredity assume spiritual and political rulership.

The Shiites teach that the religious leaders have supernatural wisdom not available to other men. They teach that these religious leaders may make decisions above the political leaders and that they must be obeyed.

Anwar Sadat of Egypt was a Sunni, of the conservative sect.

Ayatollah Ruhollah Khomeini was a Shiite, of the militant group.

Shiite Mobilizer of Jihad

In 1963 Iran was swept by riots stirred up by powerful Islamic Shiite leaders. (In Iran, 90 percent of its Moslems are Shiites.) These riots protested Shah Mohammad Reza Pahlavi's Western ways, calling him a traitor to Islam.

The Shah put down the disturbances and arrested one of its religious instigators — Ayatollah Ruhollah Khomeini.

Khomeini was exiled first to Turkey and then to Iraq. But he could not be silenced. He continued to preach against the idolatrous Shah — and for a "new nation of Islam."

His philosophy is summed up in this statement to reporters: ''Islam means everything . . . Islam contains everything. Islam includes everything. Islam is everything.''

And Islam, as we have seen, demands Jihad. Even as Khomeini sat in exile, he sowed seeds of Holy War in Iran.

He consistently cried out that the Shah and his U.S. ties must go.

The major reason for the downfall of the Shah was his opposition to his own religion — Shiite Islam — and to Ayatollah Khomeini. When it became apparent that Khomeini's followers were everywhere displaying the Ayatollah's picture, the Shah put pressure on the government of Iraq to put him out of the country.

Khomeini fled to a small village outside Paris in October 1978. And from there he broadcast his message against Western theology, taking advantage of Western technology's most modern means of communication.

He talked to the Western press.

He sent his messages into the streets of Tehran by means of cassette tapes, often sold by sidewalk vendors. These were played in the mosques and in the homes of people — every day gathering more power and strength for Khomeini and his call for a return to pure Islamic ways and goals.

He could pick up a telephone in Paris and his followers in Tehran would march in the streets. He called for strikes, shut down banks, closed factories, shops, and oil wells.

The Shah was powerless to stop it. On January 16, 1979, the Shah left the country and with it his ancestral throne ending one of the earth's oldest monarchies.

On February 1, 1979, the Imam Khomeini returned in triumph from France after 15 years as a political exile. He was met by millions of jubilant Iranians shouting, ''The holy one has come! He is the light of our lives!''

Khomeini assumed the political and religious leadership of the nation being designated as Iran's ruler until his death in 1989.

13

Islam Attacks "the Great Satan"

November 4, 1979, will go down in history as a day of infamy and shame.

Iran, the Imam, and Islam grabbed the attention of the world by attacking the U.S. Embassy in Tehran. It was beseiged and captured.

A large number of people were inside the embassy doing business that day. No high American official was present. Sixty-three American hostages were taken. Ten were released later. Fifty-three were held.

On the 156th day of the captivity of the American hostages, the United States had exhausted its patience and broke diplomatic relations with Iran. They had sought aid and assistance from every available group — the United Nations, the World Court, the Common Market nations of Europe. Nothing availed.

Most of the world does not even understand the type of war that is being waged.

Yet Khomeini made it very plain that this was Jihad.

His cries were not heard across a sandy desert plain; they were carried around the world by the twentieth century's most sophisticated media.

Only Satan could have caused him to set out upon such a dangerous course at this time in history.

Operation Eagle Claw

The desert debacle of Friday, April 20, 1980, was called Eagle Claw by the Pentagon. It was given this name to hold its secret mission. It was under the direction of Colonel Charles Beckwith.

The American government decided to recapture the American Embassy in Tehran and to free the people who had been imprisoned at that time for over half a year.

The military rescue effort was aborted in the staging area in Iran's great salt desert 250 miles from the target in Tehran.

Terrible wind storms whipped up the desert sand in unbelievable fury. The men could not see where to go.

It ended with eight U.S. servicemen left dead on the burning sands surrounded by three disabled Sea Stallion helicopters and a great C-130 Hercules transport burned to a crisp.

I personally asked God why such a nation as America with the finest equipment on the face of this earth and the best fighting men on the face of this earth should fail in a mission such as this. I prayed desperately for an answer. It was not only for me — it was for the whole Western world.

Khomeini's Cries of Jihad

"This is not a struggle between the United States and Iran," Khomeini declared. "It is a struggle between Islam and the infidels."

Here Khomeini definitely said this is not a political situation, but a religious one. All who are not Moslems are considered infidels.

"America is the mother of corruption," Khomeini stated in a speech.

Because of the strength of evangelism and Bibles being distributed from the United States, Khomeini considers this evangelical thrust as the one which gives birth to what he considers corruption.

"The United States is Enemy Number One of humanity," Khomeini said in a radio broadcast.

Khomeini made statements like this because 90 percent of all missionary dollars going out around the world to convert people to the Lord Jesus Christ come from the United States. Therefore he openly declared that the U.S. was a greater threat to him than the Russians on his north who are infidels and killers, as they showed in Afghanistan.

"Why should we be afraid?" Khomeini said of any American attempt to use force. "We consider martyrdom a great honor."

These people are the ultimate fanatics and are possessed with a desire to militantly subdue nations and take them from the true life in Christ.

In a radio broadcast, Khomeini screamed for the entire Islamic world to join him. "Join us in this struggle between the infidel and Islam!"

"All Moslems should join us," he said, "because if this revolution fails, the East and Moslem countries will be destroyed as a result."

"This is not a struggle between the U.S. and Iran," he said in another speech. "It is a struggle between Islam and blasphemy."

It is very possible the people of the Western world have not until this point identified the titanic struggle in the breast of the Moslem to destroy Christianity and Judaism off the face of the earth.

One has to go back to the Middle Ages and carefully study the terrible battles between the crusaders and the Moslems to understand this fury.

One finds it difficult to see how the flames of hatred and revolution could burn for 1,400 years unless they are satanic in origin.

Khomeini's inflammatory statements set off a rash of incidents around the world.

Strangest of all and perhaps the most likely to shock the Moslem world, 500 terrorists dressed as pilgrims attacked Islam's holiest shrine, the Grand Mosque in Mecca. A radical Moslem cult sought recognition of its leader as the Islamic Messiah. (Moslems believe a secret Imam will one day appear. There will be, according to Moslem belief, no more prophets. Mohammed was the last. But directly under the prophets are the Imams.)

Government troops reclaimed the mosque, but not before several days' fighting and several men dying.

Khomeini found a way to blame the U.S. and Israel for the attack.

An enraged mob attacked the U.S. Embassy in Pakistan. They burned our magnificent government building; two Americans were killed. Pakistani government troops rescued 100 Americans who had been trapped inside the burning building for hours.

The U.S. Consulate building in Izmir, Turkey, was stoned and windows were broken.

In Dacca, Bangladesh, mobs shouted, "Down with American imperialism!"

In Calcutta, India, our President was burned in effigy.

Khomeini was hoping to start the real Jihad. Had he been successful, there would have been the greatest religious battle the world had ever known.

Were we a first-class nation or not?

The Lord spoke back to me the same Friday that President Carter made his speech relating to the aborted raid.

If the Americans had reached the city, there would have been more bloodshed than ever imagined.

I trembled to think of this. I thought of how it might have triggered the confrontation with Russia — and how it could have been a world which would have aroused the whole of the Arab world with a Jihad such as history has no record of.

God gave the Russian world further opportunity to seek His face, repent of their sins, and ask His blessings upon their lives.

Iran with its Moslem fanatics was held at bay, the whole Western world refusing to obey international law and begging the Arab states to refuse oil to the industrial nations of the world, which could bring the most chaotic condition this world has ever known.

14

The Incredible Alliance — Islam and the Infidels

We have dealt with Iraq/Iran's long past, and somewhat with its present. We will deal now with its future.

As a nation, Iraq and Iran are the oldest among mankind. How many nations can trace their existence as a people back to the flood?

Israel, as a people, can trace their existence back to Abraham — 10 generations after the flood.

To be able to clearly identify the people of Iraq/Iran from the time of Noah and the flood, through its famous world empires — the Babylon Empire and the Persian Empire — and through its ultimate destiny is unparalleled as far as I am able to ascertain.

The Bible is the only source from which to derive this information.

We will see now what the Bible has to say about Iraq/Iran's future.

A Land Desolated

The entire world knows that for 2,000 years the land of Israel was a desolate piece of property.

What brought about the desolation of the "Promised Land?"

Abraham came up out of Ur (Iraq) of the Chaldees as God's solitary prophet leaving the sin, the idolatry, and the paganism behind. He was to go to the land of Canaan to worship Jehovah and through this seed to bring the world a Savior.

When God called Abram out of Ur, He spoke to him about a promised land.

God said:

> **Get thee out of thy country, and from thy kindred, and from thy father's house, unto a land that I will shew thee. And I will make of thee a great nation, and I will bless thee . . . .**
>
> **Genesis 12:1,2**

Later, God told Abraham how long this land would belong to his seed. **For all the land which thou seest, to thee will I give it, and to thy seed forever** (Gen. 13:15).

God specifically laid out the location of the land (Gen. 15:18-21):

> **In the same day the Lord made a covenant with Abram, saying, Unto thy seed have I given this land, from the river of Egypt unto the great river, the river Euphrates: the Kenites, and the Kenizzites, and the Kadmonites, and the Hittites, and the Perrizzites, and the Rephaim, and the Amorites, and the Canaanites, and the Girgashites, and the Jebusites.**

God made a covenant with this people through whom He would bring a Savior to all men. He promised to bless them.

Moses was very careful to tell the people of Israel, speaking with the voice of God, the blessings that were theirs if they would remember God and His precepts — and the cursings they would suffer if they did not. (Deut. 28).

Israel forgot God. They forgot His sabbaths. They forgot His commandments. They forgot all the things God had done for them. So the Word of God in Deuteronomy 28 was fulfilled.

The rising power of empire overwhelmed them and they were taken into Babylonian captivity for over 70 years.

A remnant returned — some say one-sixth — to rebuild Jerusalem. But it was never the same as it had been in the days of David.

The prophets foretold that the peoples of Israel would wander and be dispersed among the heathen. And that as a result, their land would be desolate.

It has been estimated that at the beginning of the Christian era, four million Jews lived in various parts of Europe, Asia, and Africa, while 700,000 lived in their own land.

The destruction of Jerusalem by Titus in 70 A.D. brought about the final scattering of the Jews.

When Israel followed God and occupied the land He gave them, the land showed forth His blessing. It was even called a land of milk and honey.

But when the rightful heirs were disobedient, or were gone all together, the land bore the shame of barrenness. It would never produce for anyone but its rightful owners.

A Land Revived

Ezekiel, the prophet of God, is a source of information relative to the last days of the "dispensation of grace."

In Ezekiel 36, he prophesied exactly how the land of Israel would be revived.

God Himself speaks to mountains! He requires them to change from a desolate place into a fruitful place!

Ezekiel was commanded of God to prophesy relative to the endtime saying that the mountains would shoot forth their branches — that they would yield their fruit to the people of Israel. (v. 8.)

Ezekiel prophesied that the land would again be tilled and sown. (v. 9.)

Ezekiel says that God will multiply man and beast; and they shall increase and bear fruit.

Then God, through the prophet Ezekiel, says, **I will settle you after your old estates, and will do better unto you than at your beginnings: and ye shall know that I am the Lord** (v. 11).

Through the centuries, the earth of the Promised Land has been covered with blood many times. The Crusaders fought violently there to redeem Jerusalem for the Christians. Every major empire in history played its part there. The Roman empire devastated the land. And it has been devastated many times since.

For 400 years the Turks ruled the land. They even put a tax on trees. People cut down their trees in order not to pay tax. And the land became exceedingly desolate.

But in my lifetime — in the past 25 to 30 years — God changed the land.

He brought back rain upon the soil. He caused millions of trees to be planted. The entire land today has had a rebirth from barrenness to fruitfulness.

Some of the most delicious fruit I have tasted in the world — and I have lived and ministered in over 100 countries — grows on the hillsides of Israel.

The world has watched while Ezekiel's 2,500-year-old prophecy of a land's reviving came true.

The Revival of a Nation

In the very next chapter, chapter 37, God calls the prophet Ezekiel to prophesy relative to a nation.

He had prophesied to the waste places. He had prophesied to the desolate ground. And now the Spirit of God takes him to a valley full of dry bones.

God asked the prophet, **Son of man, can these bones live?** (v. 3).

Ezekiel was so astounded at the sight of the bleached bones in the desert, that he had to say, **O Lord God, Thou knowest** (v. 3).

In all the universe, God was the only one who believed that He could gather men from more than 100 countries of the world and cause them to fit into one body to become a strong nation.

Listen to what God told Ezekiel to prophesy to the scattered bones: **Prophesy unto these bones, and say into them, O ye dry bones, hear the word of the Lord. Thus saith the Lord God unto these bones; Behold, I will cause breath to enter into you, and ye shall live . . . and ye shall know that I am the Lord** (vv. 4,5).

Ezekiel obeyed God. He prophesied to the bones. Then he watched them come together, stand upon their feet, and become an exceeding great army (v. 10).

Then God told Ezekiel who the bones were: **Then he said unto me, Son of man, these bones are the whole house of Israel** (v. 11).

God said, **I will take the children of Israel from among the heathen, whither they be gone, and will gather them on every side, and bring them into their own land: And I will make them one nation in the land upon the mountains of Israel . . .** (vv. 21, 22).

In our lifetime, we have seen the Israeli people come from the four corners of the earth. We have watched them assemble themselves in their old places and build a nation with such vigor and passion that with less than four million of them, they could challenge 100 million neighbors.

Incredible! Yet all knowledgeable observers agree this has already been accomplished and that this miracle has been performed in our times.

Again, the prophet Ezekiel in two successive chapters has met the test of a true prophet — his prophecies have been fulfilled.

Now we come to the next two chapters of Ezekiel — 38 and 39 — where we see one of the most astounding prophecies of history.

This next prophecy of Ezekiel has been written about — it has been much discussed — and it is very near completion. It gives the prophetic future of the ancient nation of Israel. But it also gives the prophetic future of the ancient nations of Iraq/Iran and the not-to-distant future of the USSR.

For the Sake of Jihad!
Iraq/Iran Joins with Infidel

Again, Ezekiel is told to prophesy.

> Son of man, set thy face against Gog, the land of Magog, the chief prince of Meshech and Tubal, and prophesy against him.
>
> Ezekiel 38:2

We can identify to whom God refers by going back to Genesis chapter 10 where the generations of the sons of Noah are given. Japheth was one of Noah's three sons.

> The sons of Japheth; Gomer, and Magog, and Madai, and Javan, and Tubal, and Meshech, and Tiras.
>
> Genesis 10:2

Magog, Tubal, and Meshech were grandsons of Noah. They settled north of the Black Sea and east. This is the land Ezekiel 38:2 names.

Most teachers of Bible prophecy clearly identify the combination of Soviet alliances to be these people. Moscow, in the west, and Tobolsk, in the east, of the Soviet Union are clearly recognizable.

What does Ezekiel prophesy to them?

> After many days thou shalt be visited: in the latter years thou shalt come into the land that is brought back from the sword, and is gathered out of many people, against the mountains of Israel, which have been always waste: but it is brought forth out of the nations, and they shall dwell safely all of them.
>
> (v. 8)

God identifies a time — in the latter years.

In the latter years, northern lands shall come down upon Israel, a people brough back from the sword. Israel — a persecuted people for 2,000 years — would be attacked from the north in their own land where they had come to dwell safely.

> Thou shalt ascend and come like a storm, thou
> shalt be like a cloud to cover the land, thou, and all
> thy bands, and many people with thee.
>
> (v. 9)

These people from the north shall come possibly
in a larger military force than the world has ever before
witnessed.

> . . . thou shalt think an evil thought: And thou
> shalt say, I will go up to the land of the unwalled
> villages; I will go to them that are at rest, that dwell
> safely, all of them dwelling without walls, and having
> neither bars nor gates.
>
> (v. 11)

Such a thing was unheard of in the time Ezekiel
wrote this. There were no such cities. There were no
such towns. All towns had walls around them to
protect the residents from wild beasts and hostile
armies. They all had gates. They all had bars.

This was a prophecy that would not be understood
by the people in Ezekiel's day, 600 years before the
Lord Jesus Christ was born.

They will come for a spoil. Read the thirty-eighth
and thirty-ninth chapters of Ezekiel for the complete
picture of a war before it is fought.

Now, let's go back a bit. Verse 9 said to Russia,
all thy bands and many people with thee.

Who will come down with Russia against Israel?

Verses 5 and 6 name the allies. The first one is
named Persia.

> Persia, Etheopia, and Libya with them; all of
> them with shield and helmet.
>
> (v. 5)

Persia — modern Iraq/Iran.

Ethiopia — North Africa.

Libya — Eastern and North Africa, or it could be an area south of Kush in the area of Syria and Iran.

Other allies are mentioned in verse 6 — but the ones we have named would know the meaning of Jihad.

The Jihad! The Holy War! And Persia will be leading the way in this battle.

Iraq and Iran may be destined to join the atheists and Moslems of Russia — the communists of Russia — to come against Israel. Only in madness would this thing be conceived. Only in anger of the deepest sort could it be brought forth.

These people who believe that Allah is the one true god, will join with the Moslems and infidels of Russia who do not believe in God, to come against Israel whose father is Abraham.

The World News

No doubt the world news in the near future will give an amazing broadcast like this:

"Ladies and gentlemen: We have very bad news to report. Millions of Moslems have joined with their Soviet brothers in a march upon Israel. The U.S. and Israel have moved into the oil reserve nations of Arabia and have captured them. Israel and the U.S. must be stopped, otherwise Israel will control the entire world. Therefore, the united armies which include most of the Arab states, with the exception of Egypt and Jordan, are marching against Israel tonight.

"Ladies and gentlemen, by tomorrow morning, there will be no Israel. So many of these people are marching south, it seems like a cloud. The sun is hardly visible with the dust that rises from this mightiest army of all mankind. This is Israel's last night on this earth as the nation of Israel. Tomorrow morning it will be no more."

The Next Day

The following day the world news reports will be as follows:

"Ladies and gentlemen: There is a surprise in world news. Yesterday it was forecast that today Israel would no longer be a nation. But from our reporters in that area, we have learned that a strange phenomenon has taken place.

"Israel is very much alive! But Russia and its allies are dead!

"At this moment we are not able to explain this. We are only able to say that very strong radio and television stations out of Jerusalem are inviting the entire world to come to Israel. Millions are dead. Israeli officials are asking visitors to bring a shovel. Anyone can keep all the riches they may find on any body they will bury. Officials have predicted it will take seven months to bury all the dead. (Ezek. 39:12.) Long live Israel!"

This is what a broadcast may sound like after it happens.

God forecast it 2,600 years before it happens. And just as certainly as Ezekiel chapter 36 came to pass regarding the restoration of the land — and just as certainly as Ezekiel chapter 37 came to pass regarding the coming together of the peoples from dispersion — Ezekiel 38 and 39 will come to pass in full.

God foretold that "in the latter days" those who have fought against Him and denied Him, and those who agree to walk with them, will die on the vast plains of Megiddo in northern Israel.

God Himself will fight against those people who come against Israel:

> I will plead against him with pestilence and with blood; and I will rain upon him, and upon his bands, and upon the many people that are with him, an overflowing rain, and great hailstones, fire, and brimstone. Thus will I magnify myself and sanctify (honor) myself; and I will be known in the eyes of many nations, and they shall know that I am the Lord.
> Ezekiel 38:22,23

> And it shall come to pass in that day, that I will give unto Gog a place there of graves in Israel, the valley of the passengers on the east of the sea: and it shall stop the noses of the passengers: and there shall they bury Gog and all his multitude: and they shall call it The valley of Hamangog. And seven months shall the house of Israel bury them, that they may cleanse the land.

> Yea, all the people of the land shall bury them; and it shall be to them a renown the day that I shall be glorified, saith the Lord God.

> And they shall sever out men of continual employment, passing through the land to bury with the passengers those that remain upon the face of the earth, to clease it: after the end of seven months shall they search.

> And the passengers that pass through the land, when any seeth a man's bone, then shall he set up

a sign by it, till the buriers have buried it in the valley of Hamangog.

Ezekiel 39:11-15

God sums up the situation in Ezekiel 39:28,29:

Then shall they know that I am the Lord their God, which caused them to be led into captivity among the heathen: but I have gathered them unto their own land, and have left none of them any more there. Neither will I hide my face any more from them: for I have poured out my spirit upon the house of Israel, saith the Lord God.

Iraq/Iran, nations which had the witness of God in the miracle of the News salvation during the years of their Jewish Queen, Esther . . .

Iraq/Iran, nations which had the witness of wise men . . .

Iraq/Iran, nations which had the witness of the people who were at the first outpouring of the Holy Spirit and the birth of the Church . . .

Iraq/Iran, who despite all that, chose Islam and Jihad, will find devastation and desolation on the plains of Megiddo.

15

God's Answer to Jihad
(The Holy War)

Our earth has known great wars. It has known much bloodshed. But after the final war, the day of peace will come.

Closing out the great tribulation, Jesus Christ will return to personally fight against the Antichrist and his armies to destroy them.

A prophecy we have already looked at foretold it. One of the most outstanding prophecies of the entire Bible is the vision the first world empire builder saw. Let's look at it again, this time paying particular attention to the last part:

> **Thou, O king, sawest, and behold a great image. This great image, whose brightness was excellent, stood before thee; and the form thereof was terrible.**
>
> **This image's head was of fine gold, his breast and his arms of silver, his belly and his thighs of brass, his legs of iron, his feet part of iron and part of clay.**
>
> **Thou sawest till that a stone was cut out without hands, which smote the image upon his feet that were of iron and clay, and brake them to pieces.**
>
> **Daniel 2:31-34**

This is the final Jihad.

A Stone would be cut without hands from the mountain. This Stone is Jesus. He is the Rock of Ages.

He is the Smiting Stone. He is the Cornerstone of all civilization.

He was cut without hands. He was born of a virgin. He did not come to this earth as other men had come. He came as the Son of God to redeem the world from its sins. He was not promoted to a place of authority by any human instrument. He had no natural assistance in making him the King of kings and the Lord of lords. The Stone was cut without hands.

God says this Stone smote the image upon his feet which were of iron and clay and brake them to pieces.

Because that's the time in history in which He strikes. The Stone without hands does not smite in the time of the gold, or the silver, or the brass. He smites in the last days of this world's empires.

The Stone strikes the ten-toed kingdom of the Antichrist, which is very likely being brought into existence today through the Common Market countries of Europe.

This ten-nation confederacy will choose a fateful leader. That leader will befriend Israel and make a seven-year covenant with her after she has defeated Russia.

At the destruction of Russia as a world power, the next great power will be that of the Common Market countries of Europe. They will be the richest and most powerful of all nations. Already they exhange products with no import tariffs.

From these nations shall rise the Antichrist. He will accuse God of all earth's problems. And forces under his leadership will war with God.

At that point, the Stone will smite the feet of this great image God spoke of so many years before.

> **Then was the iron, the clay, the brass, the silver, and the gold, broken to pieces together, and became like the chaff of the summer threshingfloors; and the wind carried them away, that no place was found for them: and the stone that smote the image became a great mountain, and filled the whole earth.**
>
> **Daniel 2:35**

How could the gold, the silver, the brass, the iron, and the clay be broken in pieces "together" when they are so many ceturies apart?

What all these empires stood for still remains today. Each contributed its part to the chaotic conditions of today's world.

1. Babylon/Iraq. It was in Babylon that the occult came into its power. Superstitions were born there. Babylon was the nesting place of spiritism, demonism, Satanism. The occult offspring of Babylon constitute one of the greatest problems in the world today. When that Stone which is cut without hands smites the image, Babylon will forever be defeated with all of its occult, sinister, nether-world teachings. All spiritism will completely die when Babylon is struck down by the Lord Jesus Christ.

2. The Persian Empire/Iran. The Persian empire represents indulgence. It represents every lust of the human flesh. It represents luxury at its highest. The very spirit of the Persian courts is in the world today, strongly anti-God, and destroying virtue. All of the sins of the great Persian courts are on our highways and streets to this day. All the lewdness of our modern world has the spirit of Persia in it. And that Stone, when it comes, will smite and destroy these sins.

3. The Grecian Empire/Europe. Greece represents learning — philosophy — man without need for God. Humanism is its strength. This empire remains with us today. It stalks down our university halls. It screams over the mass media saying that man is sufficient. He does not need God. He is acceptable in his own rights. Man can make a way for himself. When the Lord Jesus comes, He will smite this. The whole world shall know that God is God, and that Christ is the Savior of the world.

4. The Roman Empire/USA. The Romans represented the people's government. "Let the will of the people be done," they said. The great power of Rome is with us today in the democracies of the world, saying, "With government we can save ourselves. We can make laws to correct ourselves. Government is the answer."

I was in a Florida court room when the judge said, "In this room law is God."

I was astounded. I responded, "Judge, nowhere on earth is law God." He did not listen.

Rome with all of its fantasies and assumed power failed. All human governments around the world have failed miserably. When that Stone smites them, they shall be broken in pieces.

The next few words of that prophecy are very significant. These empires — these achievements of man — shall become like the chaff of the summer threshingfloors. The wind will carry them away. No place will be found for them. When the Lord Jesus Christ shall rule over this earth for 1,000 years, there will be no memories of these despotic empires which sought to rule man and the world.

God would have you realize that things of this world will pass away. The cults of Babylon, the luxury of Persia, the learning of the Greeks, the government of the Romans shall all be swept away. God says they will be like chaff. They will be as nothing. They will be blown away. The wind carries them away and no place is found for them. Forever they are gone from the memory of man.

The last line is wonderful!

The Stone that smote the image became a great mountain and filled the whole earth!

The Lord Jesus Christ shall become King of kings and Lord of lords! He shall become Master of all mankind.

The last Jihad is when our Lord and Master becomes supreme upon the earth and destroys from it all forces of evil. He is the Conquering One who sets humanity free!

Revelation 17:14 describes that war: **These shall make war with the Lamb, and the Lamb shall overcome them: for he is Lord of lords, and King of kings: and they that are with him are called, and chosen, and faithful.**

The final battle will be between the forces of Antichrist against the power of the Lord Jesus Christ.

Details of the battle are already foretold. Its outcome is already decided. God revealed through His

servant John that at the conclusion of the great
bloodbath, Jesus has destroyed His enemies.

A multitude cries out!

> **And I heard it as it were the voice of a great
> multitude, and as the voice of many waters, and as
> the voice of mighty thunderings, saying, Alleluia: for
> the Lord God omnipotent reigneth.**
>
> **Revelation 19:6**

There shall be a time when the Lord Jesus gathers
His own redeemed unto Himself. They shall have a
time of rejoicing when the Lord Jesus shall be forever
united with His own.

> **Let us be glad and rejoice, and give honor to him:
> for the marriage of the Lamb is come, and his wife
> hath made herself ready.**
>
> **And to her was granted that she should be
> arrayed in fine linen, clean and white: for the fine
> linen is the righteousness of saints.**
>
> **And he saith unto me, Write, Blessed are they
> which are called unto the marriage supper of the
> Lamb. And he saith unto me, These are the true
> sayings of God.**
>
> **Revelation 19:7-9**

All those who are with the Lord shall be called
together with Him.

> **And I saw heaven opened, and behold a white
> horse; and he that sat upon him was called Faithful
> and True, and in righteousness he doth judge and
> make war.**
>
> **His eyes were as a flame of fire, and on his head
> were many crowns; and he had a name written, that
> no man knew, but he himself.**
>
> **And he was clothed with a vesture dipped in
> blood: and his name is called The Word of God.**

And the armies which were in heaven followed him upon white horses, clothed in fine linen, white and clean.

And out of his mouth goeth a sharp sword, that with it he should smite the nations: and he shall rule them with a rod of iron: and he treadeth the winepress of the fierceness and wrath of Almighty God.

And he hath on his vesture and on his thigh a name written, King of kings, and Lord of lords.

Revelation 19:11-16

This is the consummation of all Jihad!

There shall be no more wars. They shall cease.

There shall be no more tyranny. It shall cease.

There shall be no more anger. It shall cease.

16
Countdown to Armageddon

We have looked at the long history of Iraq and Iran and talked about their relationship to the plans of God in the earth and their ultimate future. But where did this all really begin, and how can we be so certain that the fate of the world will be played out on a stage in the Middle East? How do we know that the war in Iraq is not the final battle of Armageddon talked about in the Bible? To better answer those questions, let us go back to the beginning of recorded history and see the events God placed in motion that are coming to completion in this generation.

I recently took a group to visit Israel, and we traveled to the plain of Megiddo, and stood on what is called the tel of Megiddo, a hill where excavations have been done and past civilization remains can be seen. Standing there gives one such an awesome since of history. Surrounding the area are the remains of twenty different civilizations. Almost every empire in history has marched through this plain with legions of armies.

First came the Egyptians, then the Syrians, the Babylonians, Persians, Greeks and Romans. Napoleon came to the area and called it the most perfect area for war in the world. It is the area the Apostle John called Armageddon, the place of the last great conflict of good against evil, where Satan and his forces are finally defeated and overthrown.

The Biblical city of Nazareth, where Jesus grew up, is in this area. His life of thirty-three years would not be the end of His operation on the planet earth. He could look out over the valley and see the place where He would fight the last great battle with the Antichrist.

As I stood there that day with the group I was leading, the whole valley was peaceful. The grain had been harvested and the ground was ready for planting. The tourists were moving through and life was proceeding without a care. But we are people of the future. What will finally happen in this peaceful valley?

That's why I titled this chapter, "Countdown to Armageddon." But I don't think we can talk about a countdown to Armageddon without going back to the beginning where the countdown began.

When Adam, the federal head of the human family, deliberately and willfully transgressed and rebelled against the Most High God, rebellion and sin entered the human race. God began a countdown to the day that sin would have to be dealt with and destroyed.

God's first countdown began with Adam and went to Noah, where the sinful race was destroyed and Noah and his family alone were saved. But man still had the sin nature in him which God could only remove through entering the human race in the person of Jesus to redeem man and prepare for the last countdown to the final defeat of Satan and Death.

To understand this better, let us look back to Genesis 1:26, where God said, **Let us make man in our own image, after our likeness: and let them have dominion over the fish of the sea, and over the fowl** of the air, and over the cattle, and over all the earth, and over every creeping thing that creepeth upon the earth.

Genesis 2:7 tells us, **And the Lord God formed man of the dust of the ground, and breathed into his nostrils the breath of life; and man became a living soul.**

What I want to show you very positively is that there are no dark spots in history. We know the beginning of man. We know the origin of man. We know how God in His excellent majesty created man. When you get to heaven you will find that God has a nose and two eyes, just like the Bible says. It says that God created man in His own image and likeness, and placed him in a beautiful garden called Eden. And he saw that man was alone, and made a companion for him from his side and placed her in the garden with him.

But in that garden, man rebelled against his maker and sin entered the world. When Adam sinned, he planted a seed of rebellion against Jehovah in his own family. Adam's wife, Eve, conceived and bore them a son, named Cain, and a second son, named Abel. Cain tilled the ground and Abel kept sheep.

All was well in the family until the seed of rebellion Adam planted sprung up in his firstborn son, Cain. Adam knew how to worship God, because he had been taught by Jehovah himself. But Cain had a spirit of rebellion and refused to worship God as he had been taught. When jealousy rose up against his brother Abel, Cain became the first murderer.

After Abel died and Cain was cursed, Adam had a third son to take Abel's place. His name was Seth. Seth lived 105 years and had a son named Enos. At this time, Adam was 235 years old. We see the third geneation come along, still in rebellion against God.

So if you follow the generations from Adam to Noah, you will see that there were ten generations. But if you look at the years each one lived, you will see that Methuselah was born when Adam was 687 years old, and Methuselah died when he was 969 years old, the year Noah went into the ark. (Gen. 5:3-27.) Since Noah was 600 years old when he went into the ark, (Gen. 7:6.), Methuselah lived on the earth with Adam for 243 years and with Noah for 600 years. Looking at it this way, there was only one person between Adam and Noah.

Why should we be concerned with when all these people lived? It shows that God is not haphazard, but very specific in His countdown to judgment on the human race. When we look at the spiritual aspects of these generations we see that God was doing the best He could to preserve the human race and stop the terrible judgment they were bringing on themselves. But He discovered that man, through the fall of Adam, had rebellion in his blood, and it would take the supernatural intervention of God in human form to irradicate the sin nature.

Rebellion is in man's blood. Every time God prepared a way, something good for man, then man rose up with rebellion, stirred up and directed by Satan, causing him to come against God and His goodness and faithfulness. Satan hates man, who God created in His image, and constantly tries to corrupt the earth and mankind through the sin nature he introduced when man first rebelled against God, so that mankind would be lost.

The great flood was God's first judgment on sinful man. We can learn from the events in Genesis how God operates when He brings judgment. He saw the sin in Adam, and saw it continue in Adam's firstborn son, Cain, who was the first murderer. Then the human race became more and more depraved until God looked and saw that every imagination of man's heart was evil continually, and it grieved God that He had made man. (Gen. 6:5,6.)

God was ready to destroy all men and beasts in the earth, but Noah found grace in the eyes of the Lord. (Gen. 6:8.) Because one man, Noah, was righteous before God (meaning that he lived before God with all of the integrity of his knowledge of God at that time), God was able to save the human race from total destruction.

But that destruction did not come hastily. Noah spent 120 years building the ark and preaching to the world that judgment was coming, but no one, not even his father and grandfather, listened.

Jesus said in Matthew 24:3-8 that in the end times there would be wars, famines, pestilences and earthquakes in many places. God will give fair warning that judgment is coming and people need to repent and be saved before the final judgment comes on the earth.

Nearly two thousand years passed between the creation of Adam and the flood that covered the earth in Noah's day. The Bible tells of only two or three righteous men in all that time, yet God stayed His hand of judgment until the earth was totally corrupt.

One of the righteous men in that period was Enoch, the great-grandfather of Noah. Enoch was a prophet of God who preached righteousness and warned of the judgment to come. (Jude 14,15.) God warned the people over and over that judgment was coming, but nobody listened.

Two thousand years ago, God sent His Son, Jesus, to live as a man and be the perfect, sinless sacrifice for our sins. God wanted to provide a way for man to come back into fellowship with Him and stop being in bondage to Satan and sin. Jesus died so that the human race could be saved and not have to face another terrible judgment like the flood.

But man has deliberately gone away from God for these past 2,000 years. I believe that God's countdown to judgment began about 1900 (when the latter rain began) and that from the early part of this century, God began His countdown to Armageddon. (James 5:7.)

Just think of how the world has changed since 1900. Knowledge has increased in all areas of life. But more important has been the spiritual revival that began in 1900 and has swept over the entire world.

God still rules in the affairs of nations. We spent years and billions of dollars trying to protect ourselves from Communism, and God brought the Soviet Union to its knees and broke up the empire almost overnight by withholding bread. In recent years we have seen an unprecedented opportunity to preach the Gospel to the spiritually starved people in Russia and Eastern

Europe who have come free from the Communist stranglehold.

So God still has His door of grace and mercy open to the world. The time of the end is drawing near, but we are still in the countdown. Now the world can see that the focus of world events is on the Middle East and Israel, and that focus will remain until the countdown is complete and Jesus returns.

Jesus said in Matthew 24:36 that no man knows the day and hour of the Lord's return, but the Father only. Then He said that it would be just like the days of Noah — that people would be eating, drinking, marrying and carrying on business as normal.

Noah preached for 100 years. The last 100 years in our lifetime has seen the greatest advances in science and learning in the history of the world, and the greatest worldwide revival in history. God is sounding the warning that judgment is coming, and crying for people to repent and turn to Him before it is too late.

But of much of it goes in one ear and out the other. People look derisively at some television preachers and think they are just money raisers. They don't hear what's being preached.

We permit rebellion in our schools and immorality in our society, killing the unwanted babies through legalized abortions. God won't allow that to go on unchecked. judgment is coming and we are on the countdown to Armageddon, but the opportunity for repentance is still here.

Is the war in the Middle East Armageddon? No. But this war is the beginning of the fulfillment of the prophecy of Ezekiel chapters 38 and 39. We will see more earthquakes and pestilences, and the Antichrist will arise and establish his headquarters in Jerusalem and set himself up in the temple as god.

That's when Jesus will come, and His saints with Him. Then we will see the grand finale of man's rebellion against God. The carnage and destruction will be so terrible that the blood will fill the whole valley up to the horse bridles. (Rev. 14:20.)

Friends, that is the bad news. The good news is that a Savior has come, and the door of grace and mercy is still open on the earth. Let us spend our time and money and prayers and work to reach the five billion people on the earth and tell them that they don't have to perish in this great and terrible judgment on sin and rebellion.

Jesus said it would be like the days of Lot when the Son of Man returned. Lot separated himself from Abraham and went to Sodom, a city of sin and depravity. His daughters intermarried with the Sodomites, and God had to rescue Lot from Sodom when judgment came. Lot got out alive, but he lost his wife and all his possessions.

Millions of Americans have separated themselves from the Church and the faith of their fathers, and the countdown toward judgment is coming to them. In my lifetime I have seen many individuals that rebelled against God and suffered his judgment. Adolf Hitler thought he would rule the world for a thousand years, and he burned in his bunker under Berlin.

The Antichrist will soon arise in the earth, thinking he will rule forever. God will draw the whole earth together in a last great battle of death and destruction in the land of Israel at Armageddon. As sure as the Bible is true, that judgment is coming.

But you don't have to be a part of it. God is calling on man, His creation, to repent and come to Jesus and be saved from the wrath to come on the earth. He is calling His Church to be busy telling the good news about Jesus to a world plunging headlong on the countdown to Armageddon. It is time to increase our efforts in prayer and evangelism through every possible means to warn of the coming judgment and offer the way of escape through Jesus Christ.

A Final Word

Jesus talked to His disciples about the signs of the end-time in Matthew 24, and exhorted them and us not to fear when we saw these things begin to happen, but to look up and rejoice, because our redemption is near.

I believe we are in the last of the last days, and living in the most exciting times of all history as we watch prophecy being fulfilled before our eyes and a great harvest of souls come into the Kingdom of God. Now is not the time to crawl in a hole. Now is not the time to be afraid. Now is the time to proclaim the Gospel of Jesus Christ with more vigor and persistence than ever before.

Jesus is coming back soon, but before He does the great harvest of souls must come in. The fields are white and ready for harvest. Let us pray the Lord of the harvest to send forth laborers into His harvest. (Matt. 9:38.)

Church, it is time to be in prayer for laborers, and to be willing to pick up and go when the Holy Spirit says "go!" Pray for our leaders and the leaders of all nations of the world. (1 Tim. 2:1,2.) Pray for the peace of Jerusalem. (Ps. 122:6.) Pray for Christians in every nation of the world. These are days of destiny and trying times for all who love the Lord and are called by His name. The culmination of the ages is upon us, and it is a time to be more diligent and watchful than ever before.

I challenge you to do your part in fulfilling the plans of God in the earth. Pray and evangelize. Fulfill the commission of Jesus to take the Gospel to the ends of the earth (Mark 16:15), for Jesus says that only then will the end come. (Matt. 24:14.)

Pray for the Moslem nations that the doors be opened to the preaching of the Gospel and that revival might come to those caught in this great satanic deception. God will not let twenty percent of the world's population be left without the witness of Jesus preached to them, but He has given the job to the Church.

This is our finest hour! This is not the time to be hiding in a corner, praying for Jesus to come and take us out of trouble. Jesus will come when God says it is time, but when He does come, He expects to find us busy, staying in faith and winning souls to Jesus.

Take your place in the history of mankind. Pray that we, as the church, stand up and take off the cumbersome cloaks of religion and apathy and be loosed to preach the Gospel of Jesus Christ with boldness.

I challenge believers everywhere to answer the call and commission of Jesus:

> Go ye into all the world and preach the Gospel to every creature.
>
> He that believeth and is baptized shall be saved; but he that believeth not shall be damned.
>
> And these signs shall follow them that believe; in my name they shall cast out devils; they shall speak with new tongues;

> They shall take up serpents; and if they drink any deadly thing, it shall not hurt them; they shall lay hands on the sick, and they shall recover.
>
> Mark 16:15-18

A Salvation Prayer

If you are reading this book and have never experienced a personal relationship with Jesus Christ as your Savior and Lord, I encourage you to make that decision now. Romans 10:10 says that if you confess with your mouth that Jesus is Lord and believe in your heart that God raised Him from the dead, you shall be saved. Make that confession of faith now and know the peace that passes understanding, no matter what is going on in the world around you. God bless you.

Lester Sumrall is founder and chairman of a worldwide missionary outreach, The Lester Sumrall Evangelistic Association (LeSEA). Respected throughout the world as a missionary statesman, Dr. Sumrall has raised up churches and taught the Word of God for more than 60 years. In addition, he maintains headquarters for LeSEA Global and LeSEA Broadcasting (international radio and television) in South Bend, Indiana, where he resides with his wife, Louise, and pastors Christian Center Cathedral of Praise. Also involved in the ministry are three married sons: Frank, Stephen and Peter.

Dr. Sumrall is the prolific author of more than 110 books and teaching syllabi, founder and president of World Harvest Bible College, and television host on LeSEA Alive and the Lester Sumrall Teaching Series.

A powerful and dynamic speaker, Dr. Sumrall ministers God's message with authority and takes advantage of electronic media to reach the world today. He founded LeSEA Broadcasting, Inc., which owns and operates to date eight television stations: WHMB TV-40 Indianapolis, WHME TV-46 South Bend, KWHB TV-47 Tulsa, KWHE TV-14 Honolulu, WHKE TV-55 Kenosha (Wisconsin), KWHD TV-53 Denver, KWHH TV-14 Hilo, and K2IAG TV-21, Maui, Hawaii.

A recent outreach to the world's hungry has thrust Dr. Sumrall into a new dimension of showing compassion to the far corners of the earth in response to our Lord's command to "feed the hungry." Called "The End-Time Joseph Program to Feed the Hungry," Dr. Sumrall is enlisting pastor-to-pastor support of this program worldwide. It is his belief that government alone should not shoulder the responsibility of caring for the world's homeless, hungry and needy, but that the Church is to be a responsible vehicle of Christ to suffering humanity.

To receive Lester Sumrall's
monthly magazine, *World Harvest*, write:

Lester Sumrall
P. O. Box 12
South Bend, Indiana 46624

*Please include your prayer requests
and comments when you write.*

Other Books by Lester Sumrall

The Militant Church

Overcoming Compulsive Desires

101 Questions & Answers on Demon Powers

How To Cope Series
Depression
Loneliness
Rejection
Suicide
Worry

Living Free

Miracles Don't Just Happen

Demons: The Answer Book

Run With the Vision

Ecstasy

Cup of Life

The Face of Jesus

The True Story of Clarita Villaneuva

Destroying Your Deadliest Enemy

Seven Ways Jesus Healed the People

**Available from your local bookstore
or by writing:**

Harrison House
P. O. Box 35035 • Tulsa, OK 74153

The Harrison House Vision

Proclaiming the truth and the power
Of the Gospel of Jesus Christ
With excellence;

Challenging Christians to
Live victoriously,
Grow spiritually,
Know God intimately.